THE LIBRARY OF HOLOCAUST TESTIMONIES

An Englishman in Auschwitz

The Library of Holocaust Testimonies

Editors: Antony Polonsky, Martin Gilbert CBE, Aubrey Newman,
Raphael F. Scharf, Ben Helfgott MBE

Under the auspices of the Yad Vashem Committee of the Board of
Deputies of British Jews and the Centre for Holocaust Studies,
University of Leicester

My Lost World by Sara Rosen
From Dachau to Dunkirk by Fred Pelican
Breathe Deeply, My Son by Henry Wermuth
My Private War by Jacob Gerstenfeld-Maltiel
A Cat Called Adolf by Trude Levi
An End to Childhood by Miriam Akavia
A Child Alone by Martha Blend
The Children Accuse by Maria Hochberg-Marianska and Noe Gruss
I Light a Candle by Gena Turgel
My Heart in a Suitcase by Anne L. Fox
Memoirs from Occupied Warsaw, 1942–1945
by Helena Szereszewska
Have You Seen My Little Sister?
by Janina Fischler-Martinho
Surviving the Nazis, Exile and Siberia by Edith Sekules
Out of the Ghetto by Jack Klajman with Ed Klajman
From Thessaloniki to Auschwitz and Back 1926–1996
by Erika Myriam Kounio Amariglio
Translated by Theresa Sundt
I Was No. 20832 at Auschwitz by Eva Tichauer
Translated by Colette Lévy and Nicki Rensten
My Child is Back! by Ursula Pawel
Wartime Experiences in Lithuania by Rivka Lozansky Bogomolnaya
Translated by Miriam Beckerman
Who Are You, Mr Grymek? by Natan Gross
A Life Sentence of Memories by Issy Hahn, Foreword by Theo Richmond
An Englishman in Auschwitz by Leon Greenman
For Love of Life by Leah Iglinsky-Goodman
No Place to Run: The Story of David Gilbert
by Tim Shortridge and Michael D. Frounfelter
A Little House on Mount Carmel by Alexandre Blumstein
From Germany to England Via the Kindertransports by Peter Prager
By a Twist of History: The Three Lives of a Polish Jew by Mietek Sieradzki
The Jews of Poznań by Zbigniew Pakula
Lessons in Fear by Henryk Vogler

An Englishman in Auschwitz

LEON GREENMAN

VALLENTINE MITCHELL
LONDON • PORTLAND, OR

First published in 2001 by VALLENTINE MITCHELL

Catalyst House, 720 Centennial Court, Centennial Park
Elstree WD6 3SY, UK

920 NE 58th Avenue, Suite 300
Portland, Oregon 97213-3786, USA

www.vmbooks.com

British Library Cataloguing in Publication Data

Greenman, Leon, 1910–
    An Englishman in Auschwitz. – (The library of Holocaust testimonies)
    1. Greenman, Leon, 1910-2 2. Auschwitz (Concentration camp) 3. Holocaust, Jewish
    (1939)–1945) – Personal narratives, British
    I. Title
    940.5'318

    ISBN 978 0 85303 424 7
    ISSN 1363-3759

A catalog record of this book is available from the Library of Congress

Printed by CMP (UK) Ltd, Poole, Dorset

I dedicate 'The Truth' in memory of my wife Esther-Else, our baby son Barney, my sister Dinah, who voluntarily went to her death believing she was going to work in Auschwitz, our Dutch families on both sides, and all our friends. Never again Auschwitz.

Contents

List of Illustrations   viii
Biographical Note   xi
The Library of Holocaust Testimonies   xii
by Martin Gilbert
Preface   xiii
Acknowledgements   xv
Introduction   1
 1 Before the War   3
 2 The German Occupation   10
 3 Westerbork   24
 4 Birkenau   31
 5 Auschwitz – in Hospital   49
 6 Auschwitz – Camp Life   62
 7 Monowitz   71
 8 In Hospital Again   93
 9 The Death March   104
10 Buchenwald   114
11 Liberation   123

List of Illustrations

Between pages 16 and 17

1. The corner of Gun Street and Artillery Lane, East London. Leon Greenman was born on 18 December 1910, at No. 50 Artillery Lane.

2. Clara Greenman, née Morris, Leon's mother.

3. Leon Greenman's birth certificate.

4. The Jewish children of Helmersstraat in Rotterdam, 1914. Leon is in the third row, third from the left.

5. Helmersstraat in its heyday. Only one person in this picture survived the Holocaust.

6. The Zwaaf family selling ice cream at their grocery shop at No. 25 Helmersstraat in the 1930s.

7. Family group. From left to right: Leon's sister Dinah, brother Morry (who fought in the British army), Morry's wife Dolly, Leon and sister Kitty, who also stayed in Britain and survived. In order to stay with her friends the Cohens, who had been sent there, Dinah went voluntarily to Auschwitz, where she met her death.

8. Leon and Else's wedding at the East London Synagogue in Stepney on 9 June 1935. Leon's father stands next to him.

9. Leon and Else's son, Barnett 'Barney' Greenman, born 17 March 1940.

10. Esther 'Else' Greenman, née Van Dam.

11. Leon as a member of the Bram Sanders boxing school, Rotterdam, in 1938. His trained body probably saved him from the selections, which meant the gas chambers if you were too skinny and weak.

12. The Greenman family in a neighbour's garden, 1942. Shortly after this picture was taken, Jews were forbidden to visit non-

Jews, and a few months later Leon, Else and Barney were taken from their home, along with Else's grandmother.

13. Leon's identity card. All Jews had to carry one, the 'J' denoting 'Jew'.

14. Helmersstraat after bombing.

15. Letter from the Mayor of Rotterdam which states that Leon has not been called up to fight because of his English nationality.

16. Gemmeker, third from left, the SS commandant in Westerbork, standing with other officers in front of a transport (Photo courtesy Westerbork Centre).

17. A transport from Westerbork, 19 May 1944 (Photo courtesy Westerbork Centre).

Between pages 80 and 81

18. One of these huts is 'Loods 24' in Rotterdam, through which some 12,000 Rotterdam Jews passed on their way to camps.

19. Kurt Schlesinger, head of the administration department at Westerbork camp, where Dutch Jews had to assemble before being deported to concentration camps. If Schlesinger had opened his morning post before the train containing Leon and his family left Westerbork, he would have found documents relating to the Greenmans' British nationality. Schlesinger later escaped to the US, where he lived until his death.

20. The entrance to Auschwitz II – Birkenau. The trains arrived on the right-hand track. Abandoned luggage lies strewn on the other tracks (Państwowe Muzeum Auschwitz-Birkenau).

21. New arrivals at Birkenau being divided by the SS (Państwowe Muzeum Auschwitz-Birkenau).

22. Professor Horst Schumann, who experimented on Leon's body at Auschwitz. He was arrested in 1966 in Ghana, and his case came up in 1970. However, in 1971 he was set free on account of his 'illness'.

23. Else and Barney Greenman's death certificates, which state that they died 'in the region of Auschwitz' on 1 February 1943.

24. *Evening Standard* interview, April 1945.

25. Leon in the British Red Cross hospital in France, recovering from an operation on his foot. With him are his French friends, Gaston and Suzanne Pron.

26. Telegram from Leon to his sister Kitty in London, searching for information.

27. Instructions from the US Commander of Buchenwald camp for Leon, as a British subject, to be repatriated.

28. Leon shows the number that will stay with him for the rest of his life, 98288.

29. Leen Sanders, European boxing champion, who survived Auschwitz. He died in Rotterdam in the early 1990s.

30. Leon Borstrok, No. 98281, the only other survivor of the 50 men chosen from Leon's transport.

31. Leon as 'Leon Mauré' – his stage name during his years as a performer after the war.

32. Leon behind his market stall.

33. Leon as guide on one of the Anti-Nazi League's organised trips to Auschwitz, September 1996. Leon is an active participant in the ANL's work against racism.

34. Leon receives his OBE from the Queen, 24 February 1998.

Biographical Note

Leon Greenman was born in East London in 1910. His paternal grandparents were Dutch, and following his mother's death when he was 2½, the family moved to Rotterdam, where Leon grew up. In 1935 he married a Dutch Jewish woman, Esther Van Dam, and despite the rumours of war they stayed in Holland, where their son Barney was born in 1940, two months before Holland was taken over by the Nazis. Despite their British nationality, Leon, Esther 'Else' and Barney, together with Else's grandmother, were deported to Westerbork and from there to Auschwitz Birkenau, where Else and Barney met their deaths. Leon was chosen for labour and survived the camps to settle back in London, where he worked the markets and sang professionally for a living. He is now actively involved in telling new generations of the horrors of the Holocaust.

The Library of Holocaust Testimonies

It is greatly to the credit of Frank Cass that this series of survivors' testimonies is being published in Britain. The need for such a series has long been apparent here, where many survivors made their homes.

Since the end of the war in 1945 the terrible events of the Nazi destruction of European Jewry have cast a pall over our time. Six million Jews were murdered within a short period; the few survivors have had to carry in their memories whatever remains of the knowledge of Jewish life in more than a dozen countries, in several thousand towns, in tens of thousands of villages, and in innumerable families. The precious gift of recollection has been the sole memorial for millions of people whose lives were suddenly and brutally cut off.

For many years, individual survivors have published their testimonies. But many more have been reluctant to do so, often because they could not believe that they would find a publisher for their efforts.

In my own work over the past two decades, I have been approached by many survivors who had set down their memories in writing, but who did not know how to have them published. I realized what a considerable emotional strain the writing down of such hellish memories had been. I also realized, as I read many dozens of such accounts, how important each account was, in its own way, in recounting aspects of the story that had not been told before, and adding to our understanding of the wide range of human suffering, struggle and aspiration.

With so many people and so many places involved, including many hundreds of camps, it was inevitable that the historians and students of the Holocaust should find it difficult at times to grasp the scale and range of the events. The publication of memoirs is therefore an indispensable part of the extension of knowledge, and of public awareness of the crimes that had been committed against a whole people.

Martin Gilbert
Merton College, Oxford

Preface

I started my book in 1962, when I made up my mind to put on paper all I remembered of my experiences in the five Nazi concentration camps that I had survived. Every morning for about six months, before breakfast, I sat in front of an old typewriter, typing on flimsy paper, all I had at the time. Occasionally my dear landlady, Alice, asked whether she could read what I was writing about and I can still hear her words as she cursed Hitler, and her words of blessing that I had survived.

The total number of pages recounting my life in these Nazi camps became 137. Showing it to some of my acquaintances, however, it seemed they did not understand or believe what I had been through, yet I had only told the truth.

Some time later I found a ghostwriter to help me with my grammar, who wanted me to write something about my early life before the camps, and after liberation. The manuscript grew to 250 pages. Not satisfied with what the ghostwriter had added to my manuscript, I took it away; I wanted nothing else but the truth of what I had experienced. I was lucky to meet Helen Watson, who helped me with my book and made sure that I would see it on library shelves. I want the reader to know that what is written I have seen with my eyes and felt with my own body. I have added just a little from other works to make the holocaust tragedy understood, so that this will never happen again, and never be forgotten. At Auschwitz and Birkenau themselves, the truth is there for all to see, and to see is better to understand.

Leon Greenman
2001

Acknowledgements

Thank you to Helen Watson and Mick Moore for helping me get this book ready for readers 'to read and understand'. I should also like to thank Jack Kagan, who put me in touch with Frank Cass Publishers.

Introduction

'Hey there, Leon!' I turned around and wondered who was calling me. Then I saw who they were; some of my comrades from the concentration camps. 'Surprise!' I called out to them, for these were the brothers and sisters who had shared my life behind the barbed wire – a life always threatened by the SS with its military might and the ever-present possibility of death, torture and starvation. After a shaking of hands and pats on backs, my comrades asked me to come along with them to attend a ceremony to commemorate our liberation from the camps in which we were imprisoned. 'Of course I'll come along,' I said. 'Naturally I wish to be where my comrades are, among my brothers and sisters.'

Together, we walked along the road at a quick pace and then through a courtyard, between two buildings. All of a sudden, my comrades turned a corner in front of me and disappeared. I ran after them, trying to catch up, wondering why they had gone on without me. Then, as I turned the corner, I looked up and froze. A terrible shock went through me. There, before my eyes, two of my comrades were hanging by their necks. A third noose was hanging, empty, and I knew that it was waiting for me. I realised I was back in Auschwitz. In an instant, I turned around and started to run.

'Halt! Halt!' came the bellowing voice of an SS officer, but I kept on running. I raced faster and faster, all the while thinking: 'I must get away … I must get away … away from here.' The shouts of the SS officer kept ringing in my ears, commanding his guards: 'Get him! Bring him back!' They kept on running after me. They were going to catch me. They wanted to take me back to hang me. But why? Why would they want to hang me now? Europe was at peace, was it not? Germany had been defeated. I had been liberated from Buchenwald 20 years before, hadn't I? Why were they coming to hang me now, so many years later? I knew that I just had to keep running. The soldiers would shoot me in the back if I did not stop, yet I kept on running. Then I

1

realised that it was hopeless. I knew that I could not escape. They would catch me anyway, no matter how fast or how far I ran. I stopped and turned to face my pursuers. All I could see was the evil darkness in the depths of their eyes. The same evil that I had seen so many years before.

Suddenly, I was awake. There were no bullets in my back, no rope around my neck, no swinging of my body in the last moments of an agonising death. I was alive and 'free', living in London as I had for the past 20 years. In London, yes. Alive, yes. But not free. Never free of the memories and nightmares that transported me back in time, as if in a time machine. All the fear and horrors and inhumanity that I had experienced in the camps were alive in me again, as if I had never left.

It was at this moment – in the middle of the night, alone and frightened in my flat – that I realised the truth. I knew that I would never be free of the camps until I told my story. I would never be truly liberated until I honoured the promise that I had made to God on my first night at Birkenau. I promised that if God would allow my wife and child to survive this place, if he would protect me from being beaten to death or worse, if he would allow me to live through whatever horrors awaited me in this strange and terrifying place, I would do all that I could to tell the world what happened in the camps.

When I awoke from this, the most vivid of my frequent nightmares, I knew that I had to tell what I saw, what I experienced in the camps. For only then could I rest, knowing that I had kept my promise to God.

1 Before the War

Let me start by telling you of my family who came from Holland. My grandfather Isaia Groenteman was born in Amsterdam on 19 April 1828. My grandmother's name was Daatje. Isaia was an importer of goods and so it was that the Groentemans emigrated to America during the 1840s. The name Groenteman was difficult to pronounce, so Groen became Green, and the name Greenman was born. Later on, Isaia left America for England and settled in London. Here in the East End in 1876 my father Barnett, or Barney, was born. My mother's parents emigrated to London from White Russia in the eighteenth century. They escaped the pogroms and anti-Semitism, to settle in east London. Here my mother Clara Morris was born.

Barney and Clara married in the Stepney Green synagogue. I was born at 50 Artillery Lane, Whitechapel, London, on 18 December 1910. I was the fifth of six children – Daisy, Charlie, Morry and Dinah came before me, Kitty after. The time arrived that our Dutch grandparents wanted to get back to Holland, to Amsterdam. In those days, the whole family would move away with the parents to other places. My father found a house in Rotterdam, Helmersstraat, number 10a – a street made up largely of Jewish traders.

I do not remember my grandparents and I remember very little about my mother, who died in 1913 when I was two and a half. I have been told by my family that I was the apple of my mother's eye. I remember the day she died. I have a picture in my mind, of watching her falling to the floor and a lot of people standing around, coming and going. My brother Morry took me by the hand and walked me to our garden.

I later learned that my father had gone out to buy some wine and cakes for a celebration. When he turned the corner of our street, he saw a lot of people standing in front of our house. When he was told about my mother's death, he said that the wine he had bought would only be opened on the day my sister Kitty, who was only nine months old, was married. When I returned to London after the end of the war, Kitty was engaged to a Jewish soldier in the army. On her wedding day, I had the honour of opening the bottle of wine, which had been carried from place to place for all those years. It was shared among friends and family who had joined us for the wedding celebration at the home of my brother Morry.

After my mother's death, my father was left alone with six children. The strain of raising us on his own was too much, so my oldest brother Charlie who was then 16 left to join the British Army. Father sent Morry and my sister Dinah to the Jewish orphans' home at 208 Mathenesserlaan, Rotterdam. My sister Daisy went to live with friends. She later married Hyman Stad, but died at the age of 21 from a heart condition brought on by rheumatic fever. She left a nine-month-old son, Philip.

My father engaged a housekeeper, whom he later married. Stepmother Frances, as we called her, was a very strict person. Home was a clean and strict place. I cannot say that my youth was a happy one – my stepmother believed in punishing us and smacked us regularly. Once I ran away, only to be brought back by a policeman who found me asleep in a park an hour from home. The second time I ran away I went to find Morry, who was a first-class tailor working for the well-known clothing firm Kattenburg. The firm is still in existence in Rotterdam today. I spent the morning and afternoon sitting at his table and afterwards he took me home, telling me in front of our stepmother that I must behave and that no one would hit me if I did.

My life was filled with fear, and Kitty and I did not dare tell our father of the things that took place at home. The life which I led then was the overture to the life I would lead in the concentration camps. This I believe.

I remember the people who lived in our neighbourhood. Helmersstraat was a Jewish street of hard-working men and women. Some were better off than others, and some were quite poor. The families were close and helped one another when necessary. No family felt shame if they needed to borrow a cup of sugar or whatever from another family. The Polak family lived next door, above us the families Barendse, Lavino and Fresco. And I could never forget Mr van Dijk, who was often drunk and would sing and play his accordian until three in the morning. Complaining about him did no good as Mrs van Dijk was not well.

The neighbourhood children always liked to listen to my stories. We would all gather on the front steps of someone's house and I would dream up lots of adventures to entertain us all. On warm summer evenings, people would sit outside their houses at tables and chairs and play cards. At times we would see a policeman, just having a look to see that everything was all right. We always had great respect for these men with sabres at their sides.

I remember the celebrations for Queen Wilhelmina's birthday. Helmersstraat was decorated from end to end with flags, flowers, greens and all kinds of coloured lights and candles. The queen came through the streets and stood in her carriage for a few seconds, just in front of me. Since Holland's monarchs come from the House of Orange, children made orange-coloured badges which they sold for a few pennies to earn some spending money. My father was an expert at making nougat, so we would set up large planks of wood covered with clean white sheets in front of our house and sell small packets of sweets. If the weather was good and people were about, we earned some money.

My first school was at the Lijnbaanstraat, near the Kruiskade in Rotterdam. It is strange what one remembers about school. One day, I had to stand in front of the class to sing a song I had written. My headteacher was a Mr Geldhof, a wonderful calm and gentle man, and there was Miss Vijgenboom, who often smelled of urine. Mostly I remember Andje van Andel, the prettiest girl in the class. All the boys fell in love with her but she ended up marrying the teacher.

When I was 13, I left and went to a school in Mauritsstraat. My teacher was a bully who hit me more than once. I remember him smacking my face hard because I had spoiled a new piece of blotting paper. At the age of 15, I was glad to leave, looking forward to what the world had in store for me.

My stepmother bought me a pair of blue denim jeans and matching jacket for my first job, in a chocolate factory sorting bonbons covered in a white powder. I sampled them when the boss wasn't looking. When I got tired of leaving work covered in powder and had had my fill of the chocolates, I left to learn the woodworking trade at a furniture factory on the Delftsevaart.

I arrived ten minutes early for my first day there and stood in the cold, watching snow fall around me. I could see the clock in the town hall tower and, when it reached 8 o'clock, I rang the door bell. The boss lived in the flat above the factory but there was no answer. At 8.15 he came down the stairs still in his underpants. He let me in and told me to wait until the other assistant arrived. Soon I was set to work carrying blocks of wood from a large open storeroom. After a while, the owner called me over, handed me his sawdust-covered shoes and ordered me to clean them. I took some rags, cleaned and polished the shoes, and went back to carrying blocks of wood. A few minutes later, he returned, holding the shoes in his hand. He shouted at me, saying that when I was told to clean his shoes I was to use polish. I told him that the shoes were clean and shining like new. He said if I wasn't going to do what I was told, I could get my coat and cap and leave. I was there to learn a trade, not to clean shoes, so I got my things and left.

My third job was as an apprentice at Stadler and Sauerbier, a large printing firm in the Delftsestraat in Rotterdam. My duties consisted of cleaning tools and I was constantly covered in ink and gold dust. The job was not for me and soon I was unemployed.

Not long after I had left, my brothers Charlie and Morry, who were living in London, came to Rotterdam on holiday and I returned with them. Charlie made leather upholstery for furniture and Morry was a first-class tailor. Both of them later branched out, working in the markets in and around London, particularly at Petticoat Lane. I enjoyed my holiday, going to the markets with my brothers. I did not know that I would be doing the same type of work later in life.

My father wrote that he wanted me to learn a trade, so Morry arranged for me to be apprenticed to his barber who had a salon in Forest Gate. And so I started my career as a hairdresser. Six months later, father wrote to tell me of a position in his friend's salon and I returned to Rotterdam. I trained in the salon of Mr H V D Steen in the Stationsweg, a first-class barber for VIPs, doctors, solicitors and military men. I learned to use a straight razor but I was not permitted to shave customers: I practised on my father and the salon owner's bony face. After six months, I had become quite good and the owner said I should find a 'less classy' salon where I could practise cutting men's hair.

I decided that I wanted to learn ladies' hairdressing as well, so I studied at Mr de Winter's Ladies' Academy for Hairdressing for several hours every Sunday morning. Soon I was hired to work at a salon in Chrisstpijnlaan, owned by Mr Plijnaar. During my time there, my customers included championship boxer Theo Kourimsky and Councillor Gerrit van Burink, leader of the Communist Party.

After some time with Mr Plijnaar, I answered an advertisement for a position at the ladies' hair salon of Jacko Nije in Goudsestraat. During my interview, which included cutting hair, I cut a woman's ear. I rushed to get some cotton wool, managed to stop the bleeding, and apologised. When I had finished, the customer checked her hair and gave me her approval, saying that I had done just what she had asked for. I then called the boss over to see my work and, with one eye on the bandaged ear, he whispered: 'OK.' After apologising again to the customer and helping her on with her coat, I went to the boss and said goodbye, assuming that I had not been hired. He stopped me and asked why I was going. I replied that I doubted if he wanted to hire someone who had just cut a customer's ear. His reply was: 'Was it my ear? No, it was the lady's. You made your apology to her and she accepted it. Your work was good, so I want you to start work on Monday.' I worked there for two years.

While I was a hairdresser, I studied singing at the academy of music on the Mauritsweg, under Director Joseph Holthaus and the well-known tenor Cornelis van Munster. My father had told me that somewhere in the family, way back in Russia, one of my great-grandparents was a cantor in the synagogue. I wanted to become a professional singer.

I joined an amateur operatic company and the Joodse Vrienden Kring (JVK). The JVK was a circle of Jewish youth and elders. We started with a few and grew to over 100 members. Many couples married. We used to meet every Tuesday or Wednesday evening for a dance and a get-together. We rented a room in the Atlanta hotel at the Coolsingel and rehearsed for a musical entertainment once a month. (The Atlanta hotel survived the bombing of Rotterdam while all around it went up in flames.)

I became a member of the committee of the JVK and one of my responsibilities was to take visiting girls home at night. Fietje Passer, the wife of the circle's chairman Lion Passer, told me one evening that she had a girlfriend in London who was coming to Rotterdam on a holiday. She hinted that I might like her.

A few weeks later, while I was on stage taking my turn singing, Fietje walked into the club with a young girl on her arm. I was concentrating on my singing and really didn't take much notice. That evening I had about half a dozen girls to see home and the last one was Fietje's friend. I took her to her grandmother's in St Laurensstraat, we said goodnight and, after I had seen that she had locked the door, I walked home. Years later she told me that on that first night we met, she walked in and told her grandmother: 'I have found my husband to be'. I was the first boy who did not try to kiss her when he saw her home. Her name was Esther Van Dam, Else for short.

Else and I corresponded with one another after she returned to her home in Golders Green. It was mainly to be near her that I returned to London in 1930. My sister Dinah lived there and was an assistant in a pharmacist's shop. By my twenty-first birthday, I owned my own hairdressing salon in Grove Road, Bow, east London, with one full-time assistant and an apprentice to learn the trade. My petitions to them to clean and polish the waving machines or sweep the floor of fallen hair fell on deaf ears. I lost interest and the shop closed. This was the time to turn my hobby of collecting old books, prints and things from grand-mother's time into my profession; I became a partner of Else's father, who had an antiquarian bookshop in St Martin's Lane with a Mr Berkelouw. Business was steady until the Wall Street crash in 1929 and the steady stream of American tourists that made up most of our customers dried up. It was a black time for the book business. Else's family left Golders Green and moved to Brighton.

Else and I were married on 9 June 1935, at Stepney Green synagogue, where my parents and both of my brothers had been married. After the ceremony, we returned to Brighton for a cele-bration at her parents' home on the Bevendean estate. We spent our wedding night at the Blenheim Hotel, next to the Royal Pavilion. The next day we left for a honeymoon in Holland.

In Rotterdam we stayed with Else's grandmother Rosa Fransman. She lived in the Oppert, number 34. She was an old woman and asked Else to stay and look after her. As Rosa had raised her, Else agreed to stay. I divided my time between London and Rotterdam, buying and selling antique books and slowly building up my stock. Soon the house was too small, so we moved to the Harddraverstraat, number 15b.

2 The German Occupation

One day in 1938, I was leaving a booksale room in London when I noticed some men digging trenches and others issuing gas masks. At that moment, I thought: 'A war is coming.' I hurried back to Holland, with the intention of collecting Else and returning to London. Someone else in Grandma Rosa's family would have to look after her.

When I arrived back home in Rotterdam, I found Else listening to the BBC news bulletin. It was the Prime Minister Neville Chamberlain telling the world that there would be no war between England and Germany. We believed him and decided that there was no hurry to leave for England. We stayed on. Often I wished we had not believed him. Life would have been different for us.

In 1939 Else started to ask if it wasn't time to have a baby. We discussed whether or not we should – I was concerned because I believed there was going to be a war and I did not want to bring a baby into a world of such uncertainty. Else did not agree and started to cry. I gave in. Our son Barnett Greenman was born in the hospital at the Henegauwerlaan in Rotterdam on 17 March 1940. He was circumcised by the *mohel*, Mr Keizer and became a Jewish boy at the age of eight days. We registered our child at the British consulate: as both his mother and I were British subjects, he was entitled to British citizenship. While I was at the consulate, I asked about the rumours of a coming war. The staff told me they didn't know anything about it. I asked what I should do if Holland were invaded and how I should go about getting my family back to England. 'You can sign the book under Section A,' they told me. 'Which means you can leave in a fortnight's time, or under Section B, which means that you can leave in about a month. Or you can sign under Section C, which means that you will be taken back to England with our staff should they leave in the event of a war.' I signed under Section C, so that I would have a couple of months to sell the stock I had in Rotterdam.

But suddenly, on 10 May 1940, we found ourselves in the midst of war. The first bombs dropped on Rotterdam; near our home the Saint Franciscus hospital was hit even though the roof was covered with a huge red cross. I remember standing at our window, looking outside. The noise of the aeroplanes made me look upwards and I saw six bombers in a circle aiming at their targets. All of a sudden, I was pushed away from the window by the force of the falling bombs. Else was standing, bathing our baby, not yet two months old. The noise shocked her and the baby slipped out of her hands onto the floor. I turned around, picked up the baby and placed him back in his mother's hands again. We said nothing. This was our first encounter with the Nazis.

On the morning of Tuesday 14 May, I went shopping for Else. I walked towards the Zaagmolenstraat, where one of my book dealers had his shop. He was handy at binding books – I had learned a little about bookbinding from him about a year before. I thought I could add binding and repairing books to my trade. He was the kind of man who used to argue about politics and the government. Early in the afternoon, while we were talking and he was showing me how to bind a book, there came a tremendous sound above our heads. We rushed from the living room, through the passage into the shop and listened. Then we looked outside and saw a lot of smoke coming from behind the houses opposite. It was the Goudsesingel and bombs were dropping on a paper factory. I made up my mind to get to my home as soon as possible.

I ran from street to street, taking cover now and then. People were being shot at by the planes in the skies. I came to the Noordplein, then Zomerhofstraat, then Teilingerstraat and I saw people lying in the streets covered in blood, but I could not think of helping them. I had to get home to my wife and child; I was thinking all the time that our home had been bombed.

On my way, I met my friend Izak Bobbe. He cried out to me: 'Oh Leon, where are my wife and child? Look!' He showed me his bleeding hands. He had been cut by flying glass. I calmed him and told him to get to his home. I knew his wife Mimie Hart, a beautiful girl with beautiful red hair. I never saw Izak again. He was sent to the camps and never returned. Mimie still writes to me from her home in Canada.

I found myself in the Provenierstraat, taking cover from the planes. I ran a few minutes longer and then I could see our home.

The street had not been bombed and the house still stood. Quickly, I put the key in the door, opened it and ran upstairs. There I found Grandma, Else and our baby. They were crying but glad to see me. I calmed them and told them what I had seen. How much they heard and what they understood, I do not know. This was a catastrophe for us. It had come so suddenly – all at once Rotterdam was burning.

The centre of Rotterdam was totally destroyed; the city burned for four days. There was no water to put out the fires. I saw it all, walking on the hot pavements and streets. Twenty-four hours earlier I had done some shopping for my wife and now I looked at the ruins of the shops, everything in hot ashes. Old Rotterdam was no more. The Nazis had destroyed a city founded in 1200, a city with a population of over 700,000.

I went to search for my parents, who lived in the Delftsestraat. I did not find them, everything was so quiet, no one to be seen. I went back towards my home and saw lots of people lying on the grass patches near the houses. I even noticed some soldiers lying there, not seeming to know what to do. I found my parents sitting on the grass near my home, my father without a coat. They were glad to see me. I took them home and returned to the Delftsestraat to see what I could salvage for them. The fires were growing, smoke was everywhere. I found a small trolley in the street and managed to gather together some things from their home. I had to hurry: I was three storeys up in a burning building. What I ended up with was not of much value, but then who could think clearly in such circumstances? I got back home and unloaded the trolley. I went out again in search of my sister Dinah. She was not at home and it was getting dark. I turned back home, through the noise of bombs exploding and all the confusion on the streets, to find my family in a state of shock. Although we were very worried about Dinah, we were very tired and eventually went to sleep.

The following morning, I left home again to search for Dinah. I took the same route as the night before – in daylight I was able to see what was left of the streets. The Delftsestraat, where my parents lived, the Poortstraat, the Schiestraat, were hot, smouldering ruins. The heat coming from the streets became too hot for my feet and I walked to the Diergaardelaan, where I used to play among the trees, and the Stationsweg – these were no more.

From where I was standing, I could see right across to where the Helmerstraat used to be. Where the Ammanstraat used to be, where my sister's flat once stood, all these were ruins. The houses, the shops, all had disappeared, destroyed by raging fires. So this was war.

I walked further until I stood at the beginning of the Hoogstraat, a busy shopping district about a mile long, now only smouldering wreckage. Ashes and more ashes. I walked on hot bricks and pieces of concrete. It was all so unbelievable. Forty-eight hours earlier, I had walked here with friends. I saw the old mill in Oostplein, still standing. A German soldier, the first I had seen, was taking a photograph of it. I swore to myself quietly and turned back the same way. Back at home, Dinah was waiting. She had been taken in by some people the night before. I told all the family what I had seen and what was left of the centre of Rotterdam.

As time went on, we tried to live our lives as normal, but the Nazis began putting their laws and ideas into practice. Food was rationed and special laws for Jews were introduced. The first law was that all Jews had to register at the town hall, where we were asked how many Jewish grandparents we had. We were told to wear at all times a yellow star of David, on which was printed 'Jood', the Dutch word for Jew. So many people bought these stars of David at the beginning of the German occupation that some shops sold out of them. If you were unable to buy one immediately, you worried about what you would say if you were stopped.

On a trip out with Else, I remember feeling insulted when I saw a sign on the Tivoli cafe that read 'Forbidden to Jews'. I used to walk to Schiedam, two hours outside Rotterdam, to buy and sell books. It was impossible to post mail outside Holland, from where most of my business came, and no one could be reached by telephone or telegraph.

I joined with some other booksellers to go to the auction rooms of Marle, Sille & Baan in Witte de Wit Street. One of us bought books, then we took them to the ruins of the Casino theatre, where we auctioned them among ourselves. The profits were then divided between us so that we all had a little income. There were the usual well-known dealers Van Witsen, Jantje de Slechte, v.d. Sluis. One by one, the Jewish dealers were put out of business by the Germans – my bookselling days were over.

To help me earn a living, my friends who had market stalls of silk and woollen cloth handed me some remnants, sale or return. With a little attaché case, I went from house to house offering my silk or woollen cloth. Here and there I sold some, but Jewish families were being pushed out of their homes and I was not permitted to knock on the doors of non-Jews.

I started to do a bit of book binding during the mornings. One morning I met Mr Jacob Bromet, a good friend of ours from an orthodox Jewish family who lived not far from us. He told me to visit Rabbi Davids at the library in the Claes de Vrieslaan. He said that the rabbi had talked to the German occupiers, who had assured him that no harm would come to the Jews. I answered: 'I hope that this is true, but we will see.'

I made my way to the rabbi, who gave me some books to bind. I took them home and, even without the right tools, I did a good job on them and was paid well. On another occasion, the rabbi gave me a book that was very difficult to bind and I could not complete the job properly. A nasty argument ensued between myself and the rabbi. I did not see Mr Bromet again. He, his wife and two daughters were taken out of their home one night and were never seen again. Another daughter Gonnie, who was not in the house at the time, did escape. When she came home, the neighbours told her that her family had been taken away. She went into hiding with a non-Jewish family. After the war I searched for Gonnie and found her in Gouda. She was married and had had her first child. She still lives in Holland.

Jewish people were living in a state of constant uncertainty. Our circle of friends was getting smaller and smaller. Every day we heard of people being taken out of their homes and never being seen again. I had non-Jewish friends living at the Henegouwerplein, number 2a. Their son had been a student with me at the Academy of Music under Director Joseph Holthaus. It was in the days when we could still visit non-Jewish friends that Mrs van Nauta, the mother of my friend Fries, told us that, if we were taken away, we could leave Barney with them until we returned. All of our life savings, £758 in British notes, were in a safe-deposit box. We did not want this money to fall into the hands of the

Germans, so I gave it to Mrs van Nauta for safe keeping, along with our British passports.

This was a fatal mistake. I felt very bitter about what the Germans had done in bombing Rotterdam and I did not trust the Nazis. I thought that, if I were arrested, they would take the passports away and I would be without documentation of my British nationality. I am not a political man and knew nothing of international law. When the time came to collect our passports, we were informed that the van Nautas had torn up and burned them because they were afraid that the Nazis would find out they had helped Jews.

Over the next few months, I also took my most valuable antique books and prints to the van Nautas. After the war, only the remains of the less valuable books were left. I was told that the Germans had come and taken away my stock. I will never know if this was true.

Else and I made out our wills, in case anything should happen to us. We wanted our money shared between Else's younger sister Yetta, my brothers Morry and Charles in England, and my nephew Philip Stad. Some time after this, I visited the van Nautas to discuss the possibility of their taking in our child if we were taken away. This time Mrs van Nauta said: 'I am sorry but my husband is against it. The Germans might harm us for having helped you.' But we did not think badly of them, for everyone was afraid of the Nazis.

Life carried on. Jewish people had to be registered and were not allowed to visit non-Jews or go outside after 8 o'clock. We had to do what we were told. We had no radios – they had to be handed in at the police station in the Duivenvoordestraat. When I took ours in, it was checked to see if it was in good working order. When the set lit up, I noticed that it was tuned into the BBC station. I had forgotten to change the dial. At that moment the officer was looking another way; I quickly turned the knob to another station. It was strictly forbidden to listen to the outside world. Luck was with me – the voice that came from the set was not speaking in English.

We had good neighbours living in the flat above us – the family de Vos. They allowed me to come up every evening to listen to the BBC on their radio, until the non-Jews had to give up their radios too.

I had been writing to Mr Prodillier at the Swiss consulate in Amsterdam for a long time, asking for papers so we could be recognised as British subjects. Since there was no British consulate in Holland, the Swiss took over all matters concerning British citizens. They were so slow and I felt that little was being done to help us. I visited the Jewish Council. These people were responsible for sending out letters telling Jews to report for work in Germany. I did not want to work for the Germans. I was a British subject. Why did the Swiss consul take so long to answer our letters?

One evening at about 8 o'clock, the RAF flew over and dropped bombs on the city. We left our rooms and stood downstairs near the door to the street – Grandma, Else, the baby and I. The noise went on for hours and hours. At last it stopped. It must have been late at night but I opened the door and asked some people passing by where the bombing had taken place. 'All around the Henegouwerplein,' they answered. There was a school where the Nazis were housed and it was where the van Nautas lived. I took my family upstairs, saw them safe and went out to see if the van Nautas were all right.

It must have been past midnight when I made my way to the Henegouwerplein. On arrival, I found my friends knocking wooden planks against broken glass windows. I offered my help and was hammering nails when a large piece of glass fell out of the window frame and landed in my fist. The cut was deep and I made my way to the Coolsingel hospital, where I joined a long queue of others waiting to be seen. It must have been past two in the morning when I began to make my way home. It was so quiet and peaceful after all the noise but I hurried back, wondering what would happen to me if I were found. I made it home.

One afternoon, I visited the Kalkoen family. The mother was lying on the floor in hysterics because her son had received his call-up papers for Germany. Everyone was crying and downhearted – and for good reason.

Big money was being made at the photocopying shop in Coolsingel. Thousands of people copied documents there, hoping to save themselves from deportation. A lot of hope grew in that shop but it did not help. I think of this whenever I pass the Coolsingel when I'm in Rotterdam.

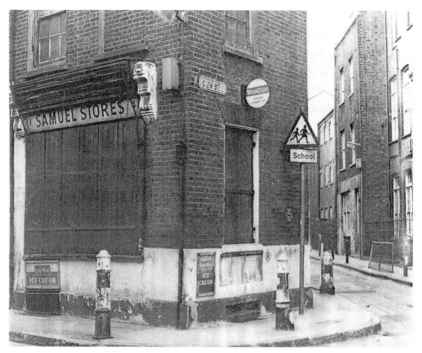

1. The corner of Gun Street and Artillery Lane, East London. Leon Greenman was born on 18 December 1910, at No. 50 Artillery Lane.

2. Clara Greenman, née Morris, Leon's mother.

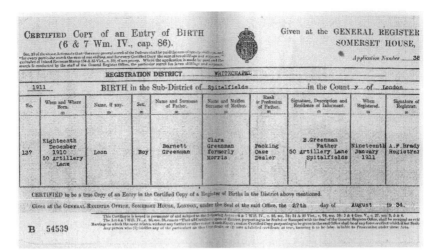

REGISTRATION DISTRICT   WHITECHAPEL

1911   BIRTH in the Sub-District of Spitalfields   in the County of London

No.	When and Where Born. (1)	Name, if any. (2)	Sex. (3)	Name and Surname of Father. (4)	Name and Maiden Surname of Mother. (5)	Rank or Profession of Father. (6)	Signature, Description and Residence of Informant. (7)	When Registered. (8)	Signature of Registrar. (9)
137	Eighteenth December 1910 50 Artillery Lane	Leon	Boy	Barnett Greenman	Clara Greenman formerly Morris	Packing Case Dealer	B.Greenman Father 50 Artillery Lane Spitalfields	Nineteenth January 1911	A.F.Brady Registrar

CERTIFIED to be a true Copy of an Entry in the Certified Copy of a Register of Births in the District above mentioned.

Given at the GENERAL REGISTER OFFICE, SOMERSET HOUSE, LONDON, under the Seal of the said Office, the 27th day of August 19 34.

B 54539

3. Leon Greenman's birth certificate.

4. The Jewish children of Helmersstraat in Rotterdam, 1914. Leon is in the third row, third from the left.

5. Helmersstraat in its heyday. Only one person in this picture survived the Holocaust.

6. The Zwaaf family selling ice cream at their grocery shop at No. 25 Helmersstraat in the 1930s.

7. Family group. From left to right: Leon's sister Dinah, brother Morry (who fought in the British army), Morry's wife Dolly, Leon and sister Kitty, who also stayed in Britain and survived. In order to stay with her friends the Cohens, who had been sent there, Dinah went voluntarily to Auschwitz, where she met her death.

8. Leon and Else's wedding at the East London Synagogue in Stepney on 9 June 1935. Leon's father stands next to him.

9. Leon and Else's son,
Barnett 'Barney' Greenman,
born 17 March 1940.

10. Esther 'Else' Greenman,
née Van Dam.

11. Leon (third from right, back row) as a member of the Bram Sanders boxing school, Rotterdam, in 1938. His trained body probably saved him from the selections, which meant the gas chambers if you were too skinny and weak.

12. The Greenman family in a neighbour's garden, 1942. Shortly after this picture was taken, Jews were forbidden to visit non-Jews, and a few months later Leon, Else and Barney were taken from their home, along with Else's grandmother.

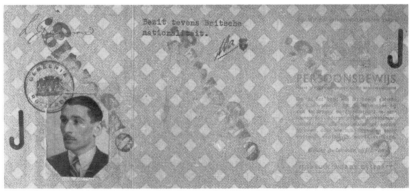

13. Leon's identity card. All Jews had to carry one, the 'J' denoting 'Jew'.

14. Helmersstraat after bombing.

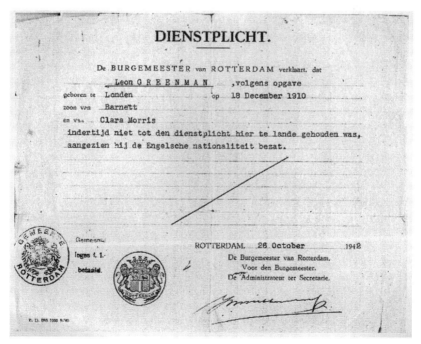

DIENSTPLICHT.

De BURGEMEESTER van ROTTERDAM verklaart, dat

_____Leon G R E E N M A N_____ , volgens opgave

geboren te Londen _____ op 18 December 1910

zoon van __Barnett

en van Clara Morris

indertijd niet tot den dienstplicht hier te lande gehouden was,

aangezien hij de Engelsche nationaliteit bezat.

ROTTERDAM, 28 October 1942

De Burgemeester van Rotterdam,
Voor den Burgemeester,
De Administrateur ter Secretarie.

15. Letter from the Mayor of Rotterdam which states that Leon has
not been called up to fight because of his English nationality.

16. Gemmeker, third from left, the SS commandant in Westerbork, standing with other officers in front of a transport (Photo courtesy Westerbork Centre).

17. A transport from Westerbork, 19 May 1944 (Photo courtesy Westerbork Centre).

Members of the Jewish community were like prisoners in their own homes. We were prohibited from most of the things we had taken for granted before the war. We were not allowed to travel by bus, tram or train, so our only mode of transport was by foot or bicycle, and the bicycles were later taken by the Germans. We could not visit cafés, cinemas, parks, restaurants or swimming pools. We were only permitted to shop between the hours of three and five, and, if Jews was caught shopping at any other time, they would be taken away.

Our lives were becoming difficult. Jewish children were not allowed to attend Dutch schools. Jewish professionals were gradually being forced out of their jobs. Slowly and steadily, businesses were closed or taken over by Nazi sympathisers. Eventually, Jews were not even permitted to have jobs. My business became impossible. Since there was no postal service between Holland and other countries I could not send books to my customers.

Even though it was forbidden to listen to BBC news broadcasts, we did so, risking punishment if we were caught. After a broadcast, I would visit friends to tell them the latest news of the Allies' efforts in the war. Many times I would knock on the door of a Jewish family only to be told by a neighbour that they had been taken away.

It helped our morale to hear that the Allies had made an advance, won a victory somewhere, however small. Afterwards, we would think to ourselves: 'Maybe they will get here soon, soon enough to keep this insanity from going any further.' But our hopes were fading daily.

My wife was more frightened than I was. Once she told me she'd heard that Jews were being gassed. I told her she was being ridiculous. Why would the Germans want to do that? I could not imagine people being killed in gas cookers, which was the only way I could imagine people being gassed. My wife was still afraid, though, and told me that, if it was true that the Germans were gassing Jews, she would rather die here at home, by committing suicide. I told her that she shouldn't even be thinking such things and tried to ease her mind, telling her that we had nothing to fear. Even though we were Jews, we were British citizens and the British government would certainly not permit anything to happen to its subjects.

Early one morning in July 1941, I learned that my sister Dinah had been taken away. She had been living with the Cohen family in Rotterdam for many years. Betje Cohen's husband was a musician and they had two children. They were called up to work in Germany, which meant deportation to the camps. Dinah felt she would be left behind, alone. She decided that if she had to work she might as well work in Germany, so she went with them, voluntarily. She, of course, did not understand what lay ahead.

In a state of shock, I rushed to the centre of Rotterdam, to the records office, to obtain documents proving my sister's British citizenship. Even though she had been born in Amsterdam, both of her parents were British, so she was entitled to British citizenship. By paying the necessary fees, I was able to obtain the documents, which I then had photocopied. I sent the citizenship documents to the authorities in a vain attempt to keep my sister from being deported.

Dinah and I had sometimes argued about the war. She was always optimistic, believing that the Allies would win the war and that everything would be all right. My reply was always: 'I agree that Germany will eventually lose the war, but what are the Germans going to do to us in the meantime? By the time the Allies win, it will be too late for most of us and for the hundreds of Jews disappearing every day all around us.' Some time later, my father received a card from Dinah, telling us that she was in Westerbork holding camp and was soon to be deported. This was the last I heard of her.

After Dinah's deportation, I became worried. She had the same citizenship as the rest of our family. If the documents I had obtained for her had not prevented her deportation, it was unlikely these documents would save the rest of us. In April 1942 I received a letter telling me to report for work in Germany. I began to panic. It was forbidden for Jews to visit the homes of non-Jews and I was afraid to go to the van Nautas to collect our passports: I could have been taken away if I was caught and the van Nautas would have been punished for helping me. Instead, I wrote a letter to the Swiss consulate in Amsterdam including application papers and photographs to obtain new British passports for me, Else and Barney.

I was always thinking about what I could do to prove our British citizenship. My friend Jo van Krimpen was a pianist and our singing quartet rehearsed with him. Jo had a job which made it possible for him to enter the town hall archives and find addresses of customers. I asked Jo to look in the archives for the papers that my father had filed, stating that all of his children were British subjects. When Jo found the card for me, I was relieved, believing at last I had a valid document which would save me from being sent to Germany. But, of course, I had to hand the card back to him so he could place it back at the town hall unnoticed.

Later, I asked the head of his department Mr de Groot to find the document where my father had declared his children's British nationality. The papers could have helped us in our predicament but Mr de Groot never wanted to listen to me or help. When I asked for him, he was never available.

A few days later, I received another letter ordering me to report for work in Germany. Again I refused to go and, as I had still not heard from the Swiss consulate, my father and I got permission to travel to Amsterdam. When we arrived at the Swiss consulate, I spoke to a secretary, Miss Jansen. After hearing my story, she said that I could take the yellow star of David off my clothes because I was British. Then I spoke to the consul Mr Prodillier. He sorted through a heap of papers on his desk until he found ours. When I asked why our documents had not been processed, he looked at me and dropped the documents back onto his desk. He told me to go home, that everything would be all right. I returned home, but received no documents from the Swiss consulate.

The doorbell rang one day, during our evening meal. I opened the door to a man in civilian clothes who said he was a police-man. He asked what nationality I was and I replied that my wife, my child and I were British citizens. I told him that I was wait-ing for documents to prove it and he ordered me to report to the police station at 9.30 the following morning. When he left, Else and I spent a very quiet evening, worrying about whether or not I would return home from the police station the next morning.

At 9.15 the next morning, I arrived at the Rotterdam alien police station at the Haagseveer. I presented myself to the recep-tion desk, sat down and waited. At the end of the corridor, I could see Chief Inspector Roos, whom I had met before. He pointed at me to follow him into a room and I was told to sit down.

He opened the conversation by telling me: 'You should be careful of the kinds of friends you have.' I didn't get his meaning, although my thoughts went to listening to the BBC news bulletins and telling war news to my Jewish and non-Jewish friends. But it wasn't that at all. He asked me about my father and what he had done during the First World War. I was too young to know or remember, but I later learned that my father had served in the Allies' intelligence service. 'You Jews do not wish to answer questions,' Mr Roos shouted. When I heard the man say 'you Jews', I guessed he was not on my side. I had to be careful here. 'What are you – British or Dutch? You have a Dutch grandfather,' he suggested. I answered that I was British and that he only had to look into the registration book to see that I arrived in Holland in 1935. 'Yes, I know you are British,' he answered. 'But I am not going up against the wall for you. I say you are Dutch as you have a Dutch grandfather.' With this, he showed me the door. This conversation was the beginning of my deportation to Auschwitz.

It was 10.15 in the evening of 8 October 1942. Our son Barney had been put to bed as usual at six o'clock. Esther and I had just gone to bed, but we were not yet asleep. We had been lying there, talking quietly about the events of the day. The RAF played a large part in our nightly conversations, for nearly every evening they could be heard flying over the city, dropping bombs. My prayers were always with them as they flew over us on their way to Germany. Most of the time, however, our nightly conversations were about our unfortunate friends and acquaintances – members of the Jewish population of Rotterdam who, day after day, were being taken from their homes or arrested on the streets by German soldiers or the police.

As we whispered together, we became sleepy and started to drop off. Then the doorbell rang. I jumped out of bed in an instant, hurried to the landing and pulled the cord to release the entry door downstairs. As I stared down from the first-floor landing, the door opened and in walked several uniformed men. One of the men shone a torch into my eyes and called out: 'Police!'

He then called my name and, when I answered, two men rushed up into our rooms. They told us to get dressed and get ready to leave the house. I tried in vain to protest to one of the men, who was dressed in a black uniform which looked like those worn by Dutch fascists. I showed him my papers from the Swiss consulate, stating that we were British subjects and were under the protection of the Swiss consulate in Amsterdam. I tried to reason with him, but he would not listen. The men told us that they had orders from the German occupation forces to come and take us from our house, and that, if my claim was justified, no doubt the commander in charge of the operation would send us home again.

Frustrated and frightened, I looked around the room and saw my wife's grandmother – a woman of 83 – trying to reason with one of the officers as her fingers nervously pulled at her clothing. My wife was standing there as well, tears streaming down her cheeks, as she told me to do as they said. I heard a sound behind me, and I turned to see Barney, standing in his cot, the cot I had made for him before he was born. He was a beautiful child with curly blond hair, blue eyes and rosy cheeks and was admired by all who saw him. He was standing, shaking the side of his cot, talking, trying to get our attention. He did not understand what was happening and wanted to be included in the conversation.

We were told to get dressed and to pack a few necessary personal items. I followed their instructions for the sake of Else who was worried that we would be hurt. What other choice did I have? I felt utterly helpless. I was on my own, with no help from my government, no help from God. I was just a Jew and, for that reason alone, a German madman had ordered us out of our home, away from all comfort and security, to an unknown destination and an unknown fate. My only hope was that, after seeing our documents, the German commander would apologise for the incovenience caused and send us home again. In my heart, I knew that this was a false hope.

The inevitable moment had come for us, just as it had for our friends and acquaintances. How does you pack for a journey with no destination? How is it possible to know what will be needed when you have no idea how long you will be gone, forced to decide in an instant what to take and what to leave behind?

I had seen it all before, always the same scene. Women screaming; mothers throwing themselves to the ground, crying and shouting; children with terrified expressions, surrounded by the bundles they had hastily packed. We had now become just one more forsaken family. In anger, I asked myself: 'Will no one stop

this insanity?' In a matter of minutes, life had become a nightmare, unnatural and surreal.

We dressed ourselves, four frightened and unhappy people.
Perhaps the baby was too young to know fear. Because of his
youth, perhaps he was spared the terror that engulfed the rest of
the family. As we were packing, the men went from room to
room, inspecting our belongings. I had several valuable books in
the apartment and one of the officers tried to convince me to
give him some of them. I told him that I would need the books
to re-establish my business when I returned. He, of course, knew
that we would not be returning home, and that our possessions
would be confiscated once we had gone. It seemed as if they were
participating in some sort of legal looting.

I thought about the long hours that I had spent finding some
of the rare editions, the happy days Else and I had spent carefully going through newly bought items and cleaning the drawings that I came across in my travels. As I watched these men
inspecting our belongings, like vultures circling their prey, I
realised that it was all being taken away – books, drawings, our
home, our clothes, furnishings, our lives.

While we were dressing, our upstairs neighbours came down,
warily at first, as German law stated that anyone found in the
home of a Jew would be arrested along with them. Our neighbours were allowed in, and tried to comfort us.

We thought that nothing would save us from deportation and
took our blankets which we had rolled up some time before and
which we were allowed to take along ready. We got together some
essentials – clothing, food and medicines packed into pillowcases
– and walked down the stairs into the street and on to a waiting
bus. A young German brownshirt shouted at us to hurry up, took
our belongings and threw them to the back of the bus. We sat in
shock as the bus drove from house to house, and watched as our
nightmare was repeated at other Jewish homes.

At around 1.30 in the morning, the coach stopped outside
large gates. The Germans began shouting, pushing and pulling
people out of the coach. I was so angry I decided that, if he
pushed Else who was holding the baby, I would push him back,
no matter the consequences, but he left us alone. Out of the bus,
we stood on the pavement, with all our belongings thrown beside

us. Our bus load had arrived at Hut 24 ('Loods 24'), the assembly place for Rotterdam's Jews.

We joined a queue which was moving towards German officers behind counters. The officers collected people's call-up forms and told them to wait. When it was my turn, I handed over my form and showed my birth certificate and letters from the Swiss consulate stating that I was a British subject. The German officer told me to show the papers to the authorities when I arrived at Westerbork, the camp my sister Dinah had been sent to.

I told Else that we would not be returning home that night as we had hoped and that we were being sent to Westerbork in the north of Holland. This was the camp from which thousands of Jews had been deported, never to be heard of again, so we were frightened and worried about our future. But there was nothing that we could do except wait and hope that someone at Westerbork would help us.

We sat down on some cases and ate a little of the food we had brought with us. After a while, I wandered around and saw many there that I knew. The time passed slowly – more and more people were arriving, carrying a few belongings, walking with shocked, defeated looks on their faces.

After two miserable days at this place, we were put onto a train in the middle of the night and sent to Westerbork. We were being sent further and further from our home and could not help wondering what was going to happen to us. My only source of hope was that we were still in Holland and I prayed that I could make someone at Westerbork understand that we were English and that all this was a mistake.

The following morning, we arrived at a place called Hooghalen. We were told to take our bundles and leave the train. There was no railway line to Westerbork camp, so we had to walk the remaining 3 miles. (Later on the prisoners of the camp helped build the track leading to Hooghalen. I can still see the men whom I knew well laying the thick, heavy, wooden poles between the rails.) It was pouring with rain and the ground was extremely muddy. Walking was difficult – Else carried the baby in one arm and a bundle in the other. I carried several and had blankets draped around my neck and shoulders. The blankets fell into the mud again and again. Grandma walked behind us as we made slow progress into the unknown.

3 Westerbork

When we finally arrived at Westerbork camp, Else and Barney were assigned to barracks for women and children with dual nationality. I was assigned to the English barrack. Couples could not sleep together. We could see one another after ten in the morning but we had to say goodnight between eight and nine in the evening.

We were registered: there was a Mr Neuburger, a German Jew, who was a lawyer by profession. He worked with Professor Meijers, the big man who had written civil laws of the Netherlands. These men were prisoners like ourselves. We talked. I showed them our documents and was told: 'We'll see what can be done for you.' I also met Westerbork's chief administrator Kurt Schlesinger, a German Jew who was very much feared in the camp. It was mainly up to him who would be deported. I asked him to place us in the hands of the Dutch Red Cross since we were British nationals. But he never did. It was difficult to approach him and talk. Six-feet tall, bald-headed and a Hitler moustache, he reigned as a dictator.

The barracks had wooden and iron bunks set up one above the other and we had to use our blankets as covers. We ate breakfast, dinner and supper at regular times and the food was not too bad. There was a large, modern kitchen and an ample kitchen staff. The camp was built by the Dutch to house German Jews who fled to Holland to escape Nazi persecution before the war. They had turned Westerbork into a little town for themselves before the Germans invaded.

Each building had a leader and everything was run according to German rules. Many of the Dutch prisoners had problems with the drills and discipline and there were lots of arguments and fights. There were too many people in the camp. It was built to hold about 1,000 people but, most of the time, there were hundreds more. There wasn't enough sleeping space and the women often argued when queuing for meals or trying to do some washing.

One day I found Else sitting on a bench with the baby in her arms. There had been no room for her in any of the bunks and the baby could not sleep in all the chaos. Once or twice a week, to make room for new arrivals, a transport of 1,000 or more Jews was sent to Auschwitz. They came and they went – the young, the old, the sick, the poor and the rich. Everyone was equal. We had little chance of escape.

I was told to report for work, but I refused to do anything to help the Germans. My friends told me that I would have to work just as they did. One day I was sent out with a working party, guarded by the SS, carrying bricks at a building site. It felt wrong working to help the enemy so, when I got back to camp, I visited the labour supervisor and told him that, as an Englishman, I would not do any work for the Germans. He said that, according to camp rules, I had to work. I became an *Essenholder*, the person who collected meals for my barrack from the kitchen.

I had to get up at 5 o'clock, take my little trolley to the kitchen, queue up with the others and take imitation coffee, tea and hot milk for people on a so-called 'special' diet to my barrack. At midday I did the same thing with a hot meal, and then again at dinner time. This job suited me well. At least I was working for my own people and not the Germans. The little extras that I got (milk or potatoes) I would share with Else, Grandma and Barney, so we all had a little more to eat.

Time passed quickly, despite the long queuing and my daily visits to the registration office. Else and I were becoming more and more desperate about our situation. But we did not give up hope of being permitted to return home.

Else's grandmother had been placed in a barracks for the sick and elderly. She was in bed and not at all well and we visited her several times a day. One day when we went to visit, we were told that she had been sent away the night before.

I met other members of my family while at Westerbork, as well as friends and acquaintances. We would talk about the deportations: and most of them said that it didn't matter whether they worked at Westerbork or in Poland – work was work. They said that at least they would still be alive. After all, work didn't hurt anybody. I couldn't understand why people were being sent to Poland to work. I wondered what they were being sent there to do.

25

In my barrack, there were many people with English–Dutch nationality. Else and I spent a lot of time with the brothers Leon and Michael Borstrock and their wives and children. One day Michael was called up for deportation. Somehow he got into the camp hospital as a patient with a stomach ulcer. He was operated on, so he stayed in the camp. A little time later, he was called up again for deportation. He was born in London, like me, so he was a British subject. To prevent the deportation, Michael tore open his stomach wound and went into hospital again.

At times, there were food shortages because there were so many people coming into the camp that the kitchen staff could not keep up. What food supplies there were were rationed among the people in the camp until a transport would leave for Auschwitz, making more room and allowing more food for those who remained and for the newcomers who arrived day after day.

In the evenings, I used to read and teach conversation English to some of the others in my barrack who had not been in England since their birth. In our own way, we all enjoyed these lessons – it gave me pleasure to be among fellow Englishmen.

There was very little chance to see Else alone during the day, as there were always other people around. This stressful period in our lives brought us closer together and, on rare occasions, we were able to meet privately after dark. She could never stay with me for very long – she was always afraid the baby would wake up. And so the nights passed, each of us hoping that help would come from somewhere. We needed it so desperately.

One day our Barney became ill. In the camp hospital barracks worked a well-known doctor called Hertzberger. He was the son of my father's doctor and friend in Rotterdam. I knew that my father visited his friend the doctor not only for paraffin oil but to have a down-to-earth political chat. When the Nazis invaded Holland, Dr Hertzberger Senior committed suicide.

Dr Hertzberger Junior took some of my blood and transfused it into Barney. I can still see it being done, with the little boy crying. We had taken him to the doctor as he had been awake all night, crying and screaming. He was put into the hospital and we had to leave him there. We were not even allowed to visit. This was difficult for us, particularly for Else, because we had never been separated from our son before. We were told that he had some sort of contagious disease of the inner ear. He was in a ward with several other children. The only way we could see him was to walk up to the window and look inside. He did not seem to recognise us. He had become very thin and pale. He could barely keep his balance and he would have to hold on to the sides of his bed to steady himself. It made me angry to see him all alone.

Our good neighbours in Rotterdam, the de Vos family, sent us food whenever they could. It was usually partially cooked brown beans that had to be warmed up. Too often, the glass jars would arrive cracked and we would have to throw the precious food away. Once we received a parcel from a cousin of mine in Amsterdam containing butter, bread amd cheese. I gave one loaf to my friends, the Wisemans, who had loaned us bread some time before.

There was a throat infection making its rounds in the camp. Else came down with it first and I followed a short time later. As we were both in bed with high temperatures, Else and I did not see one another for some time. While I was ill, I was troubled with bad dreams and confusion. We both managed to pull through and I resumed my daily visits to the camp registration office for news about our being recognised as British citizens.

One morning, when we had been at Westerbork for three months, I heard our names called on the list of those scheduled for deportation. I got dressed and went to the registration office with Mr Neuberger who had agreed to act as our solicitor. He showed the officials a letter stating that our documents were being processed and that we were due to be interned very soon. The German officials accepted the letter and our names were taken off the list. We were permitted to remain at Westerbork. Our success gave us tremendous hope.

Early one morning, a young man I knew came to my bed and told me that 200 men had been arrested from the streets in Rotterdam. The SS were at it again. At once I was up and out of bed and I dressed. I ran to the punishment prison, Barrack 51, thinking that perhaps my father was among them. It was locked up and I could not get inside. As it was still dark, I climbed up to a window, opened the top half and shouted my father's name. After a commotion inside, my father appeared at the window. We talked and I told him to stay in the barracks in the morning and that I would come and see him. I said I would take him to Mr Neuberger and that no doubt he would help my father as well.

Suddenly I felt someone pull my leg. I quickly said cheerio to my father and looked down. It was the assistant to the camp administrator Kurt Schlesinger. I heard a voice ask: 'Who is this?' It was the voice of Schlesinger himself. The assistant answered: 'It is the Englishman.' Schlesinger shouted: 'Come down immediately or I'll send you to Auschwitz.' I jumped down and stood in front of him. I told him I had not seen my father for some time and wanted to speak to him, that he could not send me to Auschwitz because I was a British national, and that my documents to prove this could arrive any moment. He looked at me as if he would beat me there and then, but he walked away.

The 200 men were set free into the camp, so I saw my father regularly. He was not in good health: I took extra hot milk to him in the mornings. Father was much more optimistic than I was about our situation. Things were not moving fast enough for me, and I did not feel happy about it at all.

By this time, Barney was out of hospital and we were all together again. He still had a low temperature and was terribly thin. Not long after his release, I was lying in bed one morning, listening to the names being announced for that day's transport to Poland when, very clearly, I heard my name, followed by Else's and Barney's. We had been at Westerbork for four months. I got up in a hurry, dressed and made straight for the registration office. But even Mr Neuberger was unable to help us this time. My protests went unheard. There would not be a second escape from deportation. Our time had run out.

I collected Else and the baby. We gathered together our bundles of blankets and a rucksack containing medicines, and waited for further instructions. It was mid-January 1943 and snow was on the ground as we stood queuing for the train. Prisoners at Westerbork had completed the rail line to the camp during our stay there, so at least we did not have to endure the long march that had brought us here. As we waited, I hoped that some miracle would happen and we would be allowed to stay.

Else was next to me, with the baby in her arms, as we slowly made our way towards the train. As we approached, I saw two men standing on the platform – SS Commander Konrad Gemmecker, the German commander of Westerbork, and Kurt Schlesinger, wearing his trademark jackboots. I told Else to go to Schlesinger and tell him about our British nationality papers. I knew that the man did not like me and thought that perhaps Else would have more luck with him.

We stopped and Else told Schlesinger that we were British subjects and we should not be leaving on the transport, since our papers were on the way so that we could be interned in Holland. Schlesinger answered: 'No, this case has been turned down by the authorities so they must be deported.' He made a gesture for us to move and turned away from us.

As we boarded the train, orders were shouted for those not leaving on the transport to go into their barracks and not come outside again. I recognised Anne Wiseman and I cried out to her: 'I'll be back.' I knew the Wiseman family very well. As a boy I used to play with Walter, Teddy and Abby, and there was Maurice. Mr Wiseman had an antiques business. Mrs Wiseman was a most kind woman; often she wasn't well. Originally the Wisemans were of Russian nationality. Mr Wiseman was with his sons in Westerbork and was deported as being without a nationality. Here again a Nazi victory. His sons were interned somehow, I never got to know how they had persuaded the Nazis to save their lives.

There were eight of us in our train compartment, sitting opposite one another in two rows. I leaned out of the window and saw one of the doctors walking along the platform. I called out to him that our child had a temperature and was too sick to travel, but he could not do anything to help us. It was nearly 11 o'clock in the morning when the train steamed out of the camp. Now all we could do was wait and see what would happen.

We had been told that we were being sent to Poland to work for the Germans. We thought that we would work during the week and be allowed to visit one another at weekends. We thought that we would get through it and start our lives anew after the war. We could only hope that the war would end soon.

During the trip, Else and I spoke of many things. We agreed that, if only one of us survived, the other would not marry again unless we found someone who would be a good step-parent for Barney, someone who would be kind to him. We talked and talked during the 36-hour trip to Poland. The train moved slowly and stopped at various places along the way. We could not see out as the windows were covered up. We were not permitted to go outside our compartment and we had nothing to drink or eat, nothing for the babies.

We slept a little, taking turns so that one of us was always awake to hold Barney. We were tired, hungry, miserable and utterly hopeless, moving to destination unknown. All that we had worked for – our business, our home and all the experiences, both good and bad, that made what we called our lives – had been taken from us because we had been born Jewish.

4 Birkenau

Eventually, the train stopped. We had arrived at a place we had never heard of before. It was Birkenau. There was silence. Then a loud voice shouted in German: 'Raus, raus! Alles lassen liggen!' Again and again, the voices went along the train. Else and I got up from our seats. We were still half asleep when the door opened and we looked out. Whatever we had been thinking could not compare to the bitter cold reality.

There were heaps of snow several feet high all over the platform, as far as the eye could see. I noticed here and there the corners of suitcases poking out of the snow drifts. I turned to Else and said that, if the snow got into the cases, it would spoil everything inside. What a waste! Why did those people leave their belongings there? Did they not need the blankets, medicines and clothing they had packed for this cold climate? Here were the cases but where were the people?

Men's voices came nearer and nearer: 'Get out! Get out! Quick! Leave all of your luggage behind.' We were shocked, bewildered, tired and not prepared to listen to these sorts of orders. I felt we had been softened up at Westerbork. We all started to move out of the train. It was a cold, dark early morning. The light was a bluish colour, or was it the moon? The lighting added to the unknown, making our way more of a mystery. There we stood on the snow-covered platform, all of our luggage left on the train. We did not need to carry anything. I thought there would be a mad rush to sort out our belongings later on. How silly!

The women were separated from the men: Else and Barney were marched about 20 yards away to a queue of women. Here I was, standing among the men, total strangers – chatting, listening and letting my eyes wander to and fro from the mass of people to my wife, to the men and back again, wondering what was coming next. Twenty yards from us were our women, our children, our mothers and sisters. I tried to watch Else. I could see her clearly against the blue lights. But she could see me too,

31

for she threw me a kiss and held our child up for me to see. What was going through her mind, I will never know. Perhaps she was pleased that the journey had come to an end. I was satisfied she was all right. We had been promised that we could meet at the weekends after our work was done. We will have a lot to talk about, I thought to myself.

Suddenly, I saw a woman run towards us – to her husband – shouting hysterically. And then, before my eyes, a big SS officer lifted his club and beat her around the head several times. Down she went, and he kicked her in the body. It was the first criminal offence I had seen and I will never forget it. Stepping over her, the SS officer came towards us and separated 50 men from the rest of the group. I was chosen. I wondered what was going to happen next.

Fifty of us had to march down the road. The women were to be taken to the bath house and those who could not walk the distance were to be given a ride in a lorry. Most of them were tired from the journey and a ride was very welcome. I could see a lorry coming our way, full of women and children. It stopped in front of us and I saw Else standing in the middle, holding our baby in her arms. I shouted her name but she could not hear me, the engine was making such a lot of noise. Else could make clothes and, from red velvet curtains at home, she had made two garments, one for Barney and one for herself. The capes covered half their bodies and rose to a point at the top of their heads. Standing out against the blue light, these two pointed hats were looking at me. The lorry moved away.

I did not know it as the lorry drove away but that was the last that I ever saw my wife and child. There would be no weekend meetings for us. I had a long and lonely life ahead of me, hard at the beginning and more and more difficult as time went on.

We 50 were marched into a barracks a short distance from the railway platform. We halted at a gate and a man behind a wire fence opened it. He asked the man leading us 'How many?' and was told 'Fifty'. The man asked: 'Why only 50? We needed 300.' 'Next transport, we will take 250 more.' The conversation made us feel like cattle or sacks of coal. The two men were prisoners like ourselves but Russians, Poles or Germans. I believed that they were going to take care of us and that we had a job to do. I figured that a job was a job and that we would most likely have the same routine as we had at Westerbork.

We entered the barracks, and then the men told us to empty our pockets or we would be beaten. But we had already lost everything at Westerbork camp. I held up my birth certificate and a letter from the Swiss consul. I wanted them to know I was English. One of them pulled the documents out of my hands and threw them to the ground. He tried to slap my face but I ducked and my eyes met the ground, which was covered with hundreds of letters, envelopes and photographs looking up at me. That's where my birth certificate landed, among the papers of the people who had arrived before us. I wondered if they felt like nobodies without their identification.

We were told to undress. Off came my wintercoat, my shoes and suit. It was a wonderful thick coat, which had been made for me in England, and had served me well. Jack Lesser, the bespoke tailor, could never have thought that his cutting and stitching would have got as far as Poland. Else had knitted a beautiful cable-stitch pullover for me – one of the Polish prisoners took it and tucked it under his own jacket. Mr Hitler, the robber. Within a few minutes, I stood in my shoes and my birthday suit and around me were 49 others dressed the same way. A bunch of naked men – ashamed, puzzled, degraded. Some of us were joking about the affair, others seemed deep in thought.

Then we were taken into another hut. I saw a few prisoners dressed in their blue and white striped camp clothing, with hair clippers in their hands. In turn, we sat upon a chair and had our heads close-cropped. All my hair came off and it was a terrible, cold feeling. No one resisted: we felt beaten. Then the hair from under my arms and the lower part of my body came off. Then, to crown it all, our heads, underarms and lower parts were soaked in paraffin. What did these fanatics think of us? We were not lousy, we were not criminals: we were clean, healthy men, just arrived from a clean country. We had come to work, not to be insulted.

After this degradation, we went into a shower room. We got under the hot and cold water when we were ordered, and tried to wash off some of the paraffin and a little of the downhearted feeling which had overtaken us. There was no soap and no towel – we had to lie down on the wooden floor to dry ourselves. After the shower, we felt a little better – some of us even started joking again. We were given a shirt, a piece of underclothing or just underpants to put on and told to sit or lie down on the wooden boards covering the ground. We looked like beggars, a comic lot, one shirt too tight, some pants too long, a tear here, no buttons there. The thick woollen blanket I had over me had a piece of linen sewn on it, with the name and address of someone in Amsterdam. I thought: 'The owner of this blanket is probably looking for it, the blanket is here. Where is he or she?' Later on, lots of things became clear to me. Lots of clothing, lorries filled to the top. Lots of luggage. It was all there, but where were the owners of these things? But it was quite warm in the bath house and some of us began to talk about our wives and children.

One or two of the bigger built Dutchmen took courage and asked the bath attendant questions about our families. The attendant – a Belgian prisoner – told us that he did not know, but we kept on trying to get information about work and our weekend meetings with the women and children. He looked at us, pointed his hand upwards: 'Heaven.' We could not make out what he meant: we thought he was fooling and trying to frighten us. We wished we would be taken elsewhere, we felt hungry and could do with a damn good sleep, if they wanted us to be fit for work.

All of a sudden, after an hour or so, we were chased out into the cold night. It was freezing and we were only dressed in ragged under-clothing. The ground was covered in snow and there was a great deal of shouting going on. Furthest away from us was a barbed-wire fence and a little hut, raised above like a look-out tower. I could just see the figure of someone moving about inside, trying to keep warm. Then I looked at the ground, a wide stretch thickly covered in snow and a mass of men, probably a few thousand prisoners, standing around being taught discipline by some uniformed prisoners.

We 50 Dutchmen stuck together as much as possible. We were being drilled to stand with five men to a row, one man behind the other. Sometimes we did not understand what the bullies wanted from us – then they would come over, kick us and drag us into the right position. This went on for quite a while and I thought that there was only one answer for this behaviour. These people were mad fanatics, showing off for the SS. I seemed to avoid the kicking and hitting, but could not help being dragged away at times, even by my own men. We were frightened and held on to one another for comfort. And it was cold, a freezing wind was going through our limbs. We were being toughened up.

Eventually we stood still in some reasonable shape although we were shivering from the cold and fright. Then there was a sound of a shot and voices shouting. We wondered if they were going to shoot us but then, against the blue of the night, I saw two men carrying a third above their heads. He was dead, shot trying to run away or caught in the barbed wire. The man was paraded in front of us. 'Any more volunteers?' we were asked. This was our warning. Try running away and you will be shot.

It must have been getting on for 5 o'clock in the morning and we had been standing outside for a considerable time now. At last, we were chased into the dozens of wooden barracks which I had not noticed earlier on because of the darkness. Inside – out of the icy cold, away from our tormentors – we were shell-shocked. How was it possible that prisoners like ourselves could share out punishment to fellow prisoners in such an inhuman way?

Inside the barracks were wooden bunks, three high; some with a few wooden boards to act as a mattress, some with none at all. We just climbed into the bunks and made ourselves as comfortable as we could. I shared a bunk with Eddie Hamel, a man I had met at Westerbork. He had been a well-known professional footballer in Amsterdam, playing for Ajax. Eddie offered to sit back-to-back to keep ourselves warm. He must have had good circulation for he was plenty warm.

Below us men were wandering around; the bunks were full of chatter, and now and then a shout – we could do with something to eat, to drink. God, we hadn't had anything for nearly three days.

We 50 Dutchmen stayed together as much as we could and many were my friends: Danzig, a violinist; Leon Borstrok, whose brother Michael tore open his stomach wound to avoid deportation; and Bargeboer from the Hague.

At last, food was carried into our barrack – large, wooden barrels filled with some kind of herb soup with black-coloured leaves. Some of the men did not like to touch it, it looked like mud or dirty water, but they had to eat something or starve. I made up my mind to eat the lot if I could, with closed eyes if I must. I had been waiting long enough and it filled my belly. Loaves of bread were also handed out, each to be shared by three men, but in the tumult that followed, the pushing and shoving, the two Poles who ought to have shared with me just disappeared and I had no bread.

As the days went by, we were drilled into some of the ways of life in a concentration camp. Do as you are told and do it quickly. If not, you got their tempers up and received a good beating. And, my God, what beatings! Before the war, I used to train at a boxing school and watched many a bout. But in the ring, the punching came from both sides. Here in the camps, it was always one-sided. You dare defend yourself and you were a dead man.

Until now I had been fairly lucky. I kept out of sight, in the background. I did not want to make myself a target. One morning I woke up with a stomach ache and an urgent need to empty my bowels. I could not wait until daylight, for there would have been a *Scheismeister* about and, who knows, a beating may have followed. I crept from my bunk, as quietly as I could, trying not to wake any of my mates. Inside the barrack, there was a wooden box on four legs in which we prisoners had to do our duty. As I neared the contraption, I noticed it was loaded to the brim. How could I go and sit on top of this dirty lot? I knew we were all being made to live an animal's life, but I had not stooped that far yet. I walked past the improvised lavatory and walked outside. I had to do the job quickly and picked a secluded spot. God only knows why, but nobody saw me go out or come in again. I got back into my bunk and fell asleep, much relieved.

All of a sudden, it was daylight. There was a lot of shouting and we were standing next to our bunks, nearly 1,000 of us. Then a fellow was brought inside: from what I could make out, he had been caught outside the barracks, doing the same thing as I had earlier on. The poor fellow got the hiding of his life – he was beaten up by the *Kapos*.

The *Kapos* were the bullies who dealt out beatings to us. Ex-professional murderers, rapists, criminals, very bad-tempered men who had been civilian prisoners for years for the crimes they had committed. The Nazis had taken these criminals out of the prisons, told them that their sentences were forgotten, taken them to concentration camps, given them a barrack with, say, 1,000 men, and told that we prisoners were bad men, brought here to be punished, work and die. So these bullies could do anything to us and the SS would not interfere. It was these fanatics we had to look out for; these were the ones who made our lives a misery. Most of them were well-built and it was no use defending yourself. You just took the beatings; you were too weak to hit back and, if you did, they would kill you there and then. We were all very frightened men.

The beatings were hard to recover from. There was always the chance that more would follow and the body, weakened by lack of food, rest and sleep, was an easy target for the strong bullies. It did not matter to them whether you lived or died: death was supposed to get you anyway, in the end.

Some of us were moved to another barrack but the 50 Dutchmen were still together. We received an extra piece of clothing each – we now had a pair of trousers and a jacket. The work we had to do passed the time. For instance, we had to turn our jackets into aprons and walk to a heap of sand where two prisoners stood. They placed two shovelfuls of sand into the jacket. Then we walked 20 yards further along and deposited the sand on the ground. We turned back to the heap and repeated the process until all the sand was at the other end of the ground. We then had to take the sand back to where we found it – the same procedure as before. Long queues of prisoners, working needlessly, all day long.

One day a Dutchman and I were told to clean up an empty barrack. Inside, the wooden bunks were all over the place and we made ourselves busy straightening them up. We were pleased to be away from the brutes and did the work slowly. As it turned out, my Dutch friend was really a German refugee who had escaped the Nazis' tyranny in his homeland and crossed over to settle in Holland. He was only young, in his twenties, and his name was Heinrich. He took one bunk, I took another. We did not talk a lot and when we did it was in a low voice. We did not want to be caught sounding as if we were enjoying ourselves.

I was busy pushing and pulling one bunk into line with the others when some of the wooden boards fell to the ground below. I picked them up and inserted them in their places. Then, before my eyes, lay a golden coin, glittering in the sunlight. I picked it up – it was a golden five-rouble piece, with the face of Tsar Nicholas II on it. It was as if it had been minted minutes before, so new and good to look at. At home this coin would have been worth anything from £20 to £30 but here, in this dump, it was worthless to me. If anybody had offered a half slice of bread for it, I would gladly have exchanged it, for bread was gold inside the camp.

I called Heinrich over and whispered what I had found. He took one look at it and said: 'Keep it, hide it away.' Perhaps I could buy food with it: there should be some greedy customer who would give me something to eat for it. It was a punishable offence to have money in the camp and I didn't want to get a hiding for it, but I put it in my pocket anyway, and hoped for the best.

I had it in my jacket pocket when I went to sleep that night, because I used my jacket as a pillow. The following morning, it had disappeared but I did not make a noise about it. Later, while we were being given an airing outside, I told my friend about what had happened. He listened but could do nothing about it. The coin did not mean very much to me: the experience of finding gold and realising that bread was more valuable meant a great deal.

We had not been allowed to wash the whole time we had been at Birkenau. We were told that the water was poisonous and that we could get dysentery. We had to make do with a small mug of white, milky-looking liquid served to us in the mornings – only a few mouthfuls in a mug, then hand the mug to your mate, for there was never enough to go round. Sometimes we did not receive fluid at all, just a little something made from flour. It wasn't oats, but it passed as breakfast. Our midday meal was half-a-dozen potatoes in their skins and a half- or a quarter-pint of watery soup. Around tea time, we sometimes got some hot herbal tea, which smelt like flowers.

Most of the time we were outside the barrack, just standing close together, trying to stay out of the wind and snow. We rubbed one another's backs, either by drawing our hands quickly up and down or by standing back-to-back and, in turn, moving up and down. Often we would get drilled, running round and round, to keep warm.

There were about 1,000 prisoners in our barrack: The wooden bunks were wide enough to sleep eight prisoners each; each bunk had three such compartments – only the top lot of men could sit up without hitting their heads and the lower spaces were only high enough to crawl in and out. But we did have wonderful woollen blankets to cover ourselves. They were the blankets of the unfortunate ones, wherever they may be.

We were out all day, from the beginning of daylight until 3.30 in the afternoon, sometimes later, depending on what time the SS officer came along to count us. We were usually up at about 4 o'clock in the morning. What a life it was, all these men standing, wriggling about, trying to get dressed. My bunk was furthest away from the lavatory, a couple of barrels that were cleaned out every day by one of our men. He volunteered for the job as it gave him an extra pint of soup a day. 'Sheismeister' was his title. The barrels were behind some curtains; there was another barrel with bleach and water for cleaning. The curses I got in the mornings, as I worked my way through the rows of men until I reached the place of deliverance, and then when I had to return.

Before we were pushed outside to get some air, the head of the barrack – the *Kapo*, or *blok alteste* as he was called – did a bunk-to-bunk inspection. The rule was that every blanket should be folded in a certain way, and all placed neatly on top of one another, just like a window carefully dressed. If one blanket was out of place, 24 men copped it, and the beatings took place. We were responsible for one another.

The same occurred in the early evening, when you went to your bunk. (We slept on wooden boards so I couldn't call it bed.) All the shoes or boots had to stand with their toes outwards, in one straight line. If one shoe happened to be out of place, the temper of the *Kapo* was roused and punishment followed. Sometimes a shoe was kicked out of position by accident so some of us kept a look out and climbed out of our bunks to put things right, to save trouble coming our way. We realised we were being held by madmen: *Kapos* did what normal human beings could not. Sleep was our best friend, for it was peaceful and we did not know where we were.

Sometimes the *Kapo* was visited by another. One evening, before getting to sleep, one of my Dutch friends called Seiz – a butcher by trade and an amateur wrestler – was called out of bed and promised some extra food if he would wrestle a tall, wonderfully fit, good-looking Pole. Thinking of the food, we looked at the game of cat and mouse they played. It was a clean, fair-enough fight, but the smaller Dutchman, who had been starved for so long, was no match for the Pole: the Pole took him so often by the neck, we wondered if his head would come off. At last, the game was over, and the Dutchman could climb back to his bunk. Perhaps he got his extra bit of food the next day. I did not notice it.

The 50 Dutchmen were wondering about their wives and children, and we asked the other *Kapos* where our families had been sent to. The answer was always the same: they pointed upwards, to heaven. But we did not believe that healthy women and children would be put to death.

It made us feel very low in spirits, so Bargeboer made a proposition, that we would not talk about the women and children while we were here, for it would send us crazy. The truth could not be found out. Why think the worst? In a little while we would probably see them again. We promised one another not to talk about our families any more.

Bargeboer did not have long to keep his feelings inside. One day he got such a good hiding, he could not get over it. He grew very thin and quiet and one morning, when we woke up, he lay dead between us. He was the first of our 50 to go. We took his frail body outside with us. He had to be accounted for when the SS officer came round for roll-call. I will never forget Bargeboer for it was a terrible thing to lose a friend like this. And yet, Bargeboer had very good boots; after his death they were given me because my shoes were finished. I wore the boots for several days but they were too small for me: my feet hurt badly. I exchanged the boots for another prisoner's shoes.

The second Dutchman to leave the group was Max Stad, my friend from Rotterdam. He had lived almost opposite our house. He was found frozen to death in his bunk – for some reason, he just gave up.

After the war, I visited his brother in Rotterdam. He told me how he continually thought of his brother Max: he knew Max had been deported but did not know what had happened to him. The silence was very worrying. I told him that I had been in the camps and, after a while, I asked him if he really wanted to know about Max and what had happened to him. He answered yes, it would stop him worrying. So I told him what I knew. He thanked me for telling him, at least there was no more uncertainty. But it was sometimes difficult to tell people what had happened, especially about a close friend.

I knew what it was like to lie awake all night, feeling the cold more than usual, when your blankets would not warm you any more and you were like a block of ice. One night I called out to our nightwatchman to do something and help me. I think I was delirious, but the following morning I was all right again. Had I been near to death? I do not know, but it was the most terrifying experience for I did not want to die, not here in any case.

One night we all were woken by a loud knocking and banging on the doors of the barrack. A voice outside was shouting 'Open up!' and our nightwatchman rushed to the door. Inside stepped a hefty SS officer, of some rank for I noticed silver braid on his uniform coat. What followed was another game of cat and mouse.

The nightwatchman was one of our own prisoners and the officer demanded to know why he had taken so long to open the door. He accused him of being asleep but the prisoner denied it. The officer took his gloved hand and let it come down on the side of the man's face, and did the same every time he denied being asleep. I saw blood coming from his nose, mouth and ears, and the beating went on for quite a while.

In the meantime, the barrack leader had left his little department and was now standing next to the accused man. Eventually the nightwatchman could not stand any longer but the officer pulled him upright and went on hitting him. The SS officer grew tired and, feeling that the common Jewish swine had got the better of him by not admitting what he had not done, told the barracks leader that he did not want to see the man ever again. And so it was to be.

Birkenau probably had more the 40,000 prisoners and many hundreds of German Gypsies, separated from us by a barbed-wire fence. We could see the Gypsy families from a distance, beautiful women and children, babies and well-built men, young and old. What had they done to be here? These Gypsies had to be fed, the same as us, and our rations of food were falling. Soon we had only two or three potatoes a day. We were very hungry and some of the Dutchmen thought it a good idea to go and see the Gypsies and ask for food. We had to be very careful so that no one would catch us.

At midday, when we had been given our miserable ration of potatoes, a few Dutchmen crawled under the barbed wire and ran to the Gypsy camp. After a few minutes, the men came back the same way and stood among us sharing out dirty potato peelings from their pockets. We ate them, even a tiny handful was satisfying to us.

I did the same thing one afternoon, crawling with a few others under the wire, keeping low to the ground and running back to the barrack: my pockets stuffed full and my cap bulging, I shared out the bits of rubbish with the others. I felt my belly become more satisfied.

But, of course, the undernourishment and the rubbish we were eating wasn't doing us any good at all. Hunger and thirst were the greatest threats, then came the beatings, in that order. Some of our fellows went as far as to drink the bleach water which they could easily get at in the lavatory. I nearly did the same but always managed to think of the consequences.

At last we were allowed to wash, but only our faces. We felt lousy, and we were. Every day, sometimes three times a day, we had to take off our shirts and search for lice – big ones, small ones and plenty of eggs. How else could it be? If the weather outside was too damp or heavy snow was falling, the barracks bully would chase us inside the barrrack and, while running up and down the warm stone fireplace, swing a stick in his hands, hitting us on the head and shoulders, to make us take off our clothes and search for lice. I found them in my torn shirt. I knew where to look, usually under the armpits in the seams. Often, as I looked at the man in front of me, I could see lice crawling on the shirt which minutes before he had inspected. What a dirty sport, killing lice with the finger nails.

One night word went around that our *Kapo* wanted some music or singing, so the Dutch violinist Danzig and I offered our art: it would give us some extra soup the following day. On several nights we were called out of our bunks to perform, while the various *Kapos* ate and drank. Soon I was known as 'the Singer'. There we stood, the Violinist and the Singer, singing and playing our hearts out, knowing that we could do with some extra food but fearing a good hiding if we did not put feeling into it.

One evening we were getting ready for sleep; everybody was in their bunks. Perhaps we felt cheated for not receiving enough rations that day but, when the *Kapo* shouted 'Gut Nacht' as usual, instead of all of us answering loudly, only a few replies were heard. The lights went out, and everybody settled down for the night. Boots and shoes were in a straight line; everybody was quiet, there was hardly a whisper. As usual, the men were tired out and longed for sleep.

About half an hour had passed when the lights were turned on and the *Kapo* shouted: 'Where are these musicians, the Singer and the Violinist?' By then, another Dutch singer had joined us so the three of us climbed down from our bunks and were told to stand by the warm fireplace as though we had to sing and make music for the bullies as usual.

Then we heard the *Kapo* shout out in a terrible temper: 'OUT OF THE BEDS'. You hear me, everybody, out of the beds. Quick, faster! Come on, faster!' While he stood watching, a few prisoners who had been picked to serve as his staff started to run up and down the barrack, along the bunks swinging sticks in their hands, hitting those who did not move quickly enough. The bewildered, half-asleep men did their best to get down on the floor as quickly as they could. They stood in silence as the new command was given: 'INTO THE BEDS, WITH YOU! Do you hear me? Everybody into the beds, quick, faster, come on, faster!' And the men started to climb into their bunks, and those who did not move fast enough, were set upon by the prisoners with sticks.

'In die bedden, aus die bedden!' It was loud and frightful. After a long time getting in and out of bed, the *Kapo* shouted: 'Nacht' and everybody answered 'Nacht' in one loud voice. The *Kapo* answered: 'That's how I want to hear it. Understood?' Now the bully sadist was satisfied.

Life went on; day after day, hunger and thirst. I would take pieces of ice from the windowsill to suck or a little grass from beneath the snow to chew. It was a way of getting something wet into your mouth, for water was scarce.

The day arrived when we were to receive our prisoner numbers. We Dutchmen clung together, even though there were no longer 50 of us because some had died and some were in the camp hospital. We were marched into another barrack and told to queue in alphabetical order. I stood at a desk behind which sat a young Jew from Austria, as he told me while writing my name, religion and place of birth on a card. He tattooed number 98288 on my left arm. I was now a number, nothing more. My name would never be used in the camps again.

The Austrian noticed I was born in England and whispered a few words to me in English: 'Whatever is asked of you, do it. Do not say you cannot, for they will make you. Don't drink the water here for it is bad and it will give you dysentery. If you get this, you will land in hospital and, depending on your body, you'll get better or not.' I understood his meaning. The hospital barrack consisted of rows of wooden bunks with broken mattresses, a few blankets and not many medicines. If your body did not heal quickly enough, the SS would not let you stay. If you were unfit to work, you went to the gas chambers. I will always remember the men outside the hospital barrack: some were tall, very tall thin creatures. They were only outside for a few minutes, with just a coat hanging around their shoulders. With the aid of a stick, they moved their long, thin legs just like skeletons. 'Muselmann', we called them. Skeleton men, ready for the gas chambers.

Our quick marches around the barracks sometimes brought us onto a road. In the distance, behind the barbed wire, I saw women and children moving about. The sight of them gave us new hope, hope that our wives and children were still alive. The fantastic stories uttered in the night about killing them off were pushed to the back of our minds. We saw the smoking chimneys, heard the tales about the crematoria, but we convinced ourselves that they were just factories.

When our labour gangs came marching back in the evenings, we could hear an orchestra playing in the distance, from Auschwitz itself. I did not know it then but in this orchestra was an old friend of mine, Louis Bannet, playing the violin and trumpet. He lived in the Helmerstraat, and we had played in the street together. When Louis came to Auschwitz, as the story goes, the *Kapo* asked for men who could play the trumpet. Three men stepped forward. The first one was given the trumpet; he blew, the *Kapo* wasn't satisfied. He gave the instrument to the second man; he blew; but the *Kapo* wasn't satisfied. He handed the trumpet to Louis, who blew the instrument to the *Kapo's* satisfaction and it saved his life, for he was taken into the orchestra. The orchestra played when we marched out in the mornings and when we marched back into the camp. But it also played music before a hanging took place. Louis and I still correspond with each other. He lives in Canada and is famous for his music making. I am proud of him, especially because so few friends survived.

We workers came back to camp in a very poor condition, some carrying our dead comrades. The weather was cold, and, with the chronic lack of food, many gave up. I made up my mind to stay alive as long as possible but one day I noticed my faeces were thin and starting to run. It was probably the beginning of dysentery, helped by the cold, and I became panicky. I thought of the little black tablets called Norit that we had brought from Rotterdam for stomach upsets. How many more people had brought medicines with them and how many thousands of pills and potions were confiscated when we arrived?

Just now I could have done with some of those Norit tablets; they would have put my stomach right. There was a rumour among our chaps that these tablets were made of special burned wood. In desperation, I burned little pieces of wood until they were black, then I pulverised them so that I could put some in soup or other fluids. Perhaps it was coincidence, but my condition did not get worse. I wanted so much to keep away from the hospital.

Once a week we had our beards shaven and our hair clipped. Sometimes I helped shave the men in our barrack. The chief barber would ask for ex-barbers, volunteers to help shave the hundreds of men in the barrack. A bit of a rush would break out, and many a man was beaten until he had picked the few to do the job. If I succeeded in having a razor or a shaving brush handed to me, I could be busy for hours on end. But it mattered not, for the pay would be an extra ration of soup, which I shared among my Dutch comrades by the spoonful. It happened that I ended up with a few more spoonfuls left in the bowl, which I drank myself. Leon Borstrock called me a scoundrel for doing so. This incident always stayed with me and I did not forget Leon Borstrock whom I met later in London a few times. (He never wanted to talk about his experiences in the camps. I remember Leon suffered from asthma when we were in Westerbork camp but somehow I never noticed his coughing.)

Our conditions were turning some of us into different people; not all of us, some remained almost the same as when they arrived. Eddie Hamel was always a gentlemen. Poor Eddie, he suffered from a large abscess inside his mouth. Others had aching feet or frostbite. My feet were starting to let me down, for I had walked in the wrong shoes, and my heels were open. They did not want to heal and, to make matters worse, the fronts of my ankles were cut by the pieces of wire I used to tie my shoes in the mornings. (My fingers were stiff from the cold and I could not tie string laces quickly enough.)

One day we were taken to another barrack – new places, new faces. We arrived and waited to be told which bunk we would be sleeping in when, all of a sudden, I heard a long cry. A prisoner was being part-carried, part-dragged along, and was placed almost before me on a low table. His face was covered in blood which was streaming from a wound on his head.

The *Kapo* stood at his side and shouted to us: 'You, the lot of you! Take notice! This man was caught going outside the doors without permission, so we did this to him. I can shoot him if I like.' And, with that, he took hold of a revolver. I thought he was going to blow the man's brains out. Luckily, he did not shoot, but all the same I wondered how long the man would take to get over this beating. The *Kapo* told us that, if we listened to him and did what he wanted us to do, he would make life bearable for us. But if we gave him trouble, he would give us the trouble we wanted – he could do what he liked with us, let us live or die.

The *Kapo* also told us that we would not be there too long, that we could be moved to the Buna, a rubber factory nearby. We did not know what to think – we were glad that we would be leaving this camp soon, get away from this hell, it could not possibly be worse elsewhere. So boys, let's be careful, we thought, stick together, and soon we'll be away from here.

Later that night, lying in my bunk, my thoughts went to the unfortunate prisoner and the beating he had received. I prayed to God not to let this happen to my wife and my family. I asked Him not to let me be beaten up or starved to death, not to allow me to become ill. If God could get me out of the camps, I promised that I would tell the outside world what I had seen inside them.

The next day, we were drilled in more camp discipline. Lots of beatings, shouting and bullying took place before our tormentors were satisfied. We had to stand five in a row, our arms stiff by our sides, fingers touching the seams of our trousers; by command, we take off our caps, and hit the sides of our legs with them. The hours we had to stand and exercise this drill! Soon it became a habit. At the end of every day, we would be inspected by an SS officer. We would be lined up and the barrack *Kapo* would shout: 'Caps off!' We would remove them and make a loud smack of a sound as they hit the sides of our legs. Then we stood motionless, faces looking out towards the front, our closely clipped hair letting the cold wind flow over our bare heads.

When the inspection was over, the SS officer walked away from us and the command 'Caps on' was given: we were allowed to go inside. Sometimes it took a long time before the command to go inside was given. We stood there, jumping up and down, to keep the circulation going, for the cold was bitter, the hunger never-ending and sleep, which took us away from this unbearable life, never sound enough.

Sometimes we had to get into our bunks having had nothing to eat or drink, but our bodies and minds got used to it. I remember the empty feeling in my belly that would not go away. Those nearest to the little room of the *Kapo* and his staff could smell them cooking their supper. But what was the use in tormenting yourself like that. It was better to turn around and try to get some sleep.

I hoped I would be strong enough to survive. My forefathers were strong men, my father, my grandfather. I often thought of it that way. Hold out to the end, you will get home again. I had to get home, back to England, to tell the folks, the outside world what was going on inside these camps, what they were doing to us. I could never keep this quiet.

We were told every day that we were going to be sent to Auschwitz. We had been in Birkenau for six weeks and we were not sorry to be leaving this filthy place, whatever may happen in the new camp.

One day we were marched into a barrack and told to take off our clothes. At the end of the room, I could see two SS officers who placed themselves on top of a table and sometimes jumped to the floor, scrutinising our naked bodies as we filed between them. One of the SS men would point to each of us with his pencil, sending us to the right, or to the left. This way the fairly strong were separated from the weak.

I stood in line and, as I reached the SS officer, someone pushed me out of the line. The officer jumped down, kicked me between the legs, and pointed me back into the queue. I could not say anything; I just felt the terrible pain and did my best to keep standing upright. I wanted to let them see that I was still strong enough to leave the camp. If I had fallen, I would not be writing this now. The skinny, weak ones, the invalids, those with wounded legs, would they go to hospital? Or would they go 'through the pipe', to die and be cremated?

As I reached the end of the queue, the SS officer pointed me to the right and I was saved. I did not follow the ones in front of me – they were weak and thin and would have to stay behind. Poor Eddie Hamel, my friend with the bad mouth, went into hospital and I never saw him again. That same evening, after roll-call, some of us were separated from the others and told to get ready to leave.

A total of 1,500 men, locking arms to form rows of five and guarded by SS soldiers with guns, we were quick-marched 3 miles to Auschwitz. We looked like groups of cattle, being chased along. When some seemed to tire, the guard was soon there to push us along. Keep going, I thought, hold onto the mates on each side of you and keep going. On and on we rushed, our breath running out. Don't let go of these arms, hold on, keep up with the rest or, who knows, the gun might speak. We were like sheep being taken to the market. My poor feet! How these small blisters can ache. Never mind, on with the race. I was alone with Polish and Czech comrades, I had lost sight of the other Dutchmen. I wondered how many of them were picked to go my way.

5 Auschwitz – in Hospital

We reached Auschwitz. We were marched into a stone building. I noticed the whitewashed walls and low ceiling. It was a large hall but too small for us, since we stood nose to nose, back to back, belly to belly – like sardines in a tin. We stood for hours like that, breathing one another's breath, feeling faint because of the warmth and the shortage of air. What the hell were they going to do with us now? This was no welcome. I had to listen to nature's call, but where to go?

We had been given a ration of bread before we left, most of us had eaten it on the way, but I held on to it. Only a little bite from the precious food had made me think: 'Who knows when I'm going to get food again? Save it until later when I'm in bed.' But now my Czech friend next to me asked whether it was bread I had under my jacket and would I like to give him some. I did so – as a matter of fact, I gave him the lot. I somehow felt ill, tired and very uncomfortable. Now that the eyes around me had seen my ration of bread, they would pinch it from me and I would rather let my friend have it. I had moments when I just could not care any more what happened to me.

At last, the door opened. It must have been very early morning and we were chased outside into the open, then into the bath-house to have a hot shower. It was lovely and refreshing, even without soap.

The following morning, 1,500 men stood on a square bit of ground, waiting, watching, looking. I was wondering what would come next. I was now alone among strangers – the Dutch-men, of whom only a few had reached Auschwitz, were some-where among the many Poles and Czechs. There was a lot of shouting and commanding going on before, at last, silence. We had to listen to what was being said. Several *Kapos* were calling out and asking what kind of professions we had; some were electricians, some painters or builders. I thought to myself:

'There'll be no room for booksellers here.' So I stepped forward and shouted the German word for hairdresser, which raised loud laughter among some of the prisoners. A *Kapo* got hold of me and pushed me into a file of men standing at the side. I could not make out what the laughter was about but, as I got to know later on, each barracks had a barber, who helped run the hut. He need not march out to work during the day and got more food. A newcomer like myself did not stand a chance of getting such a cosy job. I had been pushed into a 1,000-men commando for hard labour, such as building and digging. There were train trucks loaded with coal, to be shovelled out; loads of cement, cables, bricks, stones, iron rails, we had to carry on our shoulders.

After being registered, we received a piece of bread and sausage, and were divided into our various barracks. The outsides of the buildings looked fairly good; made of stone and bricks, they seemed very inviting compared to the wooden stables at Birkenau. But, unfortunately for me, I had to live in one of the worst. The barracks were arranged into three floors – the ground floor for more prominent prisoners, who had held a good position of trade in peacetime, the second floor for a lesser quality human being, and the third for those that came to work and die. I was to live here.

The *Kapo* of the barrack – a German madman, short and stout – would shout and lose his temper at the least thing and hand out hiding after hiding. He must have been a terrible criminal in civilian life. Our pleasures were few, and I felt very unhappy indeed. It was the same as Birkenau, where such a man could rule your life. I wished I had told a lie, that I was a painter or an electrician. Life would have been a little more bearable. Leon Borstrok, the Dutch–Englishman who came to the camps with me, mentioned that he could paint so joined another commando of men.

My *Bauhoff* commando of 1,000 men was parted into smaller units of about 100 men each. I was one of many who did the very heavy work. Perhaps the crisis was nearing for me, maybe my strength was giving out, but I felt awful. Being uncertain when this kind of life was going to end, not hearing any news of outside, a bully and his assistants to make your life miserable in the barrack, and gruelling work outside: I was miserable.

The *Kapo* of the *Bauhoff* commando was Kapo Frans, a one-armed murderer, who beat you until you could move no more.

I was terrified and I tried to keep out of his way as much as I could. The first few days, I was put to work shovelling stones and bricks into a small wheelbarrow, pushing it uphill around a bend, and emptying it out. One afternoon, I was shovelling my load when my foreman placed a large lump of stone on top of my already filled-to-the-brim barrow. The going was very difficult, one of the three wheels wasn't turning, but I kept on pushing away. If I only could get around that corner, I would feel a little safer. With great difficulty, I pushed the barrow upwards, over the brick-covered road. I felt sick and helpless. I had not much strength left but something inside was keeping me going. It would soon be time to knock off, so I held on, pushed and pushed. With great difficulty, I reached halfway up the hill, then the barrow toppled and the load came down the way I had brought it up. I looked around, expecting to hear the voice of the tormentor, and had already pictured a good hiding, but I saw nobody. I was alone and no one had seen what had happened. I had forgotten my shovel and, not caring, I got hold of my barrow and went downhill, and back to my pitch. I had escaped the arm of *Kapo* Frans.

Late that afternoon, when we marched back into Auschwitz camp we were kept outside the barracks. We had to undress and several men, who I gather were doctors, started to examine the prisoners. When it was my turn to stand in front of a doctor, he asked: 'Are you ill?' I immediately replied: 'No, I'm all right', remembering the advice I was given at Birkenau – never go into hospital.

'Let me see,' the doctor said, and he took hold of my pulse and asked to see my tongue. He looked at my feet and then he said: 'Of course you are ill. Into the hospital with you.' He was right, illness was overtaking me. How long could I go on marching and working with those feet of mine? My heels were bleeding, my ankles punctured, and I was beginning not to care any more. Everything was beyond me. If I had to die, and God wanted it, let it be!

Carrying my little bundle of clothes, I was taken to the hospital barracks, allocated a ward and shown to a bed. I stood waiting for a few minutes before I climbed in, because I didn't know whether to occupy the top or bottom bunk. From somewhere, a soft voice began calling me; I looked around, and I heard it again. It was coming from the lower bunk beside me. Someone had recognised me but I could not place the man. Seeing my puzzled face, he asked whether I had forgotten him. Not to seem impolite, I said: 'Who are you then, friend?' He answered me in Dutch: 'The barrack barber of Westerbork.'

It took a few minutes to get my mind back to Holland, so much had happened since. Then I remembered the young fellow: I used to see him often at Westerbork camp when he was cutting our hair. He looked different, his hair was short, and he looked ill. He had left Westerbork long before me so I asked him what he was doing in hospital, what was the matter with him, and how they treated the patients in here.

He didn't answer, but instead uncovered his body. He was lying on his stomach, head sideways, and what I saw I will never forget. From his hips to his back was one mass of red-, green-, black- and blue-coloured flesh. I asked him what had happened and he told me he had been beaten by a *Kapo* while at work. I only stayed on that ward for one night before I was moved. I never saw my Dutch friend again.

I received medical attention to my feet: the wounds were cleaned, covered in Vaseline and bandaged. Every other day, at about 9 o'clock in the morning, the patients who could walk had to queue for inspection of wounds. Then, in turn, we would enter a large room and receive fresh bandages. Every time I went, I noticed all kinds of men, standing with large deep wounds in their arms, legs or other parts of the body. How was it possible that human beings could stand this wear and tear? The large wounds were the result of an illness called *Phlegmone*, a swelling of parts of the body; plenty of dirty matter oozed from the large and small cuts which had been performed by the operating doctors.

Some of the men were in pain when the nurses started to clean their wounds: pieces of gauze were placed inside the wounds before they were bandaged. Later on, I understood why. The wounds had to stay open for the bad blood to get out. This must have been agonising but most of the men dare not make a sound, for the male nurses could hand out some rough stuff.

The doctor discovered the large carbuncle swelling up on my arm, and told me it had to be cut next time I came along. He took my number and put it on the list to be operated upon. I did not like the idea of lying on their table to be messed about so, when

I next went along for my fresh bandages, I left in a hurry, rushing back to my bunk to escape the operation on my arm.

Sleep overcame me when suddenly I heard my name and number being called several times. It came nearer and nearer: '98288! Greenman! Where is the Englishman 98288?' Slowly I awakened from my feverish sleep; I somehow got my head up, looked over the side of my bunk, and answered the call. 'Come down, do you not know that your arm has got to be seen to?' Dr Volmaan – a good-natured man from Poland, a prisoner like the others – was standing near my bunk. I had forgotten that he had taken down my number the other morning. There was nothing for it but to go along with him.

In the operating ward, I had to lie down on a table, my arms held backwards by a leather strap. There were no narcotics: I felt a sharp cut, and that was it. A bandage was put on and I was helped back to my bunk. Once again I gave up hope, feeling like nothing, nearing death and the end, feeling utterly hopeless, helpless and far away from everything. I was developing a temperature and was probably very ill but I did not know it. I did not want to know it.

During that period, many suffering prisoners of all nationalities came in. The bunks were now occupied by three men in each. They were really meant for one person, but two could get in lying head to toe. But now each bunk had to take three men, and it was no use grumbling about it. Nobody got much sleep – the man in the middle had to put up with the legs of the men on both sides, and the men on the sides each had one leg hanging outside the bunk. We tried to change positions, and many a nasty word was heard when tempers got out of hand or when the doctor and staff were out of the room. The poor prisoners, we were like bees in a beehive, and some of us lost our tempers. It happened to me. The three of us in my bunk had an argument, one man cursed me and, as miserable as I felt, my fist went out and I punched him. I could not have done a lot of damage, for I was weak and feverish, but my fist landed on the man's nose. He shouted out loud and the nurse came along, and asked what was going on, who was making the noise: and someone told him. I had to get out of the bunk and, with bended knees and outstretched arms, I sat for punishment in front of my bunk. For about a quarter of an hour I sat, then I was told to get back into my bunk and behave myself. It was a very light punishment, laughable compared to others I had witnessed.

Every morning at about 5.30 we used to wake up, get out of bed and wash ourselves. Then, in turn, we had to remake our beds – the thin hay mattresses and one blanket – and get back into bed and await the ration of bread and hot imitation tea or coffee. In silence I munched my bread. Some of us had a spoon or a knife to spread the margarine or to cut the bread into two or three slices, according to how thick your portion was. Then we would just try to sleep, or lie and think, or whisper little bits of gossip, or other items of news. Sleep was the finest thing for me. Away from all the trouble for a while, sometimes I would dream. Then again, if I could not get to sleep, my thoughts took me to the outside world, my family, my friends, the war and why men could do to men such things as I had witnessed.

I kept on repeating to the ward barber and the doctor that I was an Englishman, born in London, hoping again that somebody might tell somebody else and I would be sent home. It would be good to see my wife and child again. I wondered how they were getting on. What kind of work did the women have to do? But now, I could do nothing to help them. Perhaps, when I was fit again, we would meet. I could get fit if only I could get some more food. It was agony: my stomach wanted feeding but you only got your rations and that was too little to live long, too much to die quickly.

One morning I was queuing up for bandages when a man in a long coat – I presumed he was a doctor – came along the row of men and stopped in front of me. He told me to show the number on my arm: I did as requested and the man went away. I wondered what it was all about, but moved along with the queue, had my wounds cleansed and went back to my bunk.

I had noticed a slight swelling on my upper arm and told myself I had another carbuncle coming up. I started to massage it to get it to go away. I did not want to have another operation – the wounds I had were more than enough, and they did not heal.

After having put up with three men to a bed for about eight days, the doctors and staff started to move some of us to another ward. I had the top of a bunk to myself and the ward seemed brighter because the sun came in through the windows. Just beneath the windows there were two pails in a wooden box, with wooden seats, to be used when nature called. There you could catch a quick glimpse outside. I noticed there were some rabbits. I saw an SS soldier cuddling one of the rabbits. Was it possible that men could care for rabbits while their human brothers were dying from their wounds, hunger and lack of kindness?

The same night, after we had been moved to the new ward, I was awakened by the sound of wooden shoes walking down stone steps. I listened. Many steps were heard, on and on it went. There must have been hundreds of men going somewhere, but why in the middle of the night? These men were too ill to recover and so they had to be destroyed. There wasn't enough room in the hospitals; they were useless prisoners and had to make room for others to come; they were sent to the gas chambers.

There were some Dutchmen in the bunks next to me. We talked; one of them was called Groenteman. He came from the north of Holland and was a cattle dealer.

One morning, I was awakened by the sound of someone calling my number. I lifted my sleepy head and looked down over my bunk. I noticed the man who had taken my number a few days before. What could it mean? I climbed down, put on a long coat and a pair of wooden sandals and followed the man who I guessed was a doctor.

Out of the building, into another, and he showed me into a little room. I was told to sit down in a chair and wait. There was another doctor busy with some bottles; the two conversed, sometimes in French with a few words of German. I sat there. It wasn't cold, it wasn't warm, but I felt a kind of uncertainty about something. I casually asked what I was there for because I did not think myself that ill. A doctor answered: 'We are going to try a new apparatus to look inside your bladder.' I answered 'I have nothing wrong with my bladder – I have a hole in my arm, see, here. . .' I mentioned that I was a British subject, here in Auschwitz by accident. The German doctor turned around and mumbled something like: 'Oh, yes. Him.' After a while one doctor told the other that a certain person wasn't coming, and I was taken back to my bunk. I lay awake thinking about the incident, which I did not yet understand, but I sensed that not all was right.

55

The following morning the same thing happened. I was called out of my bunk by the short, fair-haired doctor in a white coat and followed him to the same little room. I sat in the same chair and thought the same thoughts. What were these men going to do? At least they could tell me. I was a patient in hospital. I had a right to know what was the matter with me. Perhaps I would be taken back to my bunk again, and they might forget about me. After a while the door opened and an SS officer in smart uniform came in. He hardly took any notice of me but he gave a command to the two doctors to commence their job.

One doctor came over to me and strapped my arms to the chair, parted my legs and strapped my legs to the chair. I could not move. The lights were dimmed and a rubber tube attached to a large glass bottle filled with liquid was placed into my penis. I felt my bladder filling up inside. There was nothing wrong with my bladder. What were they doing this for? The doctor told me to hold the liquid inside me but it was running out of me and I had to let go. The doctor told me again to hold the liquid inside me. This time, I did it, for I expected to be told off if I did not listen to them.

While the tall, dark-haired doctor was busy with me, he casually mentioned to the SS officer that I was an Englishman. The officer, who until now had not shown his face to me, turned around and faced me for a split second. I thought: 'It's now or never.' The worst that could happen to me is a good hiding but I will tell him who I am. I told him, in English, that I was a British subject, and by rights ought not to have been in Auschwitz. I said that I would like to speak to someone in authority, to help me to get out of this camp.

He answered that he was a medical officer supervising some work here and that he could not help me with my question. He advised me to take the matter up with the 'Political Department'. He spoke English with an American accent so I gathered that he must have studied there.

In the meantime, the doctors continued their work: one was seeing to an electric gadget while the tall one got busy placing an instrument, looking like a long silver pencil with a light bulb on the end, into my penis. But I had nothing the matter with my bladder. If this was God's will, then let it be so, but I was asking Him to save me, to keep me alive.

The first attempt was not successful so the doctors tried the instrument several times. Now they were really hurting me. I wasn't sick. What the hell were they trying to prove? I was a guinea pig. They were experimenting on me. I felt the instrument deep into my body. I became panicky and thought I'd never walk again. Thinking it is now or never, I shouted out: 'They are hurting me now.' I heard the SS officer say: 'Let him go, he need not come back.' I was again saved.

I was unstrapped, helped from the chair and taken back to my ward. I got back into my bunk, and lay there, thinking and falling asleep. For the next few days, whenever I answered nature's call, I had to hold on to the wall in front of me, while blood came away from my body. All the men in the bunks next to mine had to go through the same ordeal, with the same results as myself. I never found out what this experiment was for. Probably sterilisation. Could I ever make a baby again? Years after the war, I came across the SS officer's name in a book about Auschwitz experiments on prisoners. It was Horst Schumann, professor of medicine. A few years ago, I co-operated with a researcher in making a cassette recording of me telling of this experiment on my body.

I stayed in the Auschwitz hospital barrack for six weeks. The swelling in the upper part of my arm which I had managed to massage away, was now showing up at the lower part of my arm. I was desperate to get out so I showed it to one of the men helping to look after the sick prisoners. I persuaded him to remove the swelling by using a crochet needle to pierce the bump and destroy the root inside so that most of the pus came away. Somehow we succeeded in this small operation and, despite the pain, I was pleased that I need not face the knives and the table.

My wounds on my heels and ankles were now almost closed, but my arm did not want to heal up. My health was slowly improving – some days I wasn't ill enough to stay in my bunk. Then I was made to get up, walk through the ward and help the very wounded men by shaving the hair around their wounds so that they were ready to be operated upon by the doctors. If a man had a head wound, I had to shave half his head absolutely clean. This kind of work brought me some extra soup at times.

Sometimes I would shave the staff on the ward. One day a Polish nurse instructed me to give him a clean-shaven head. I did what he asked me to do but, unfortunately, my razor slipped and a little cut appeared on the blue shaven human ball under my hands. I tried to stop the bleeding – I already saw myself being kicked into the corner – why had I been so careless? I took some cold cream from the jar, and gave his head a damn good massage. It was shining like a billiard ball. It pleased him and he did not notice the cut until the next day. He did not give me any trouble. In fact, I think he took a liking to me for he often tried to make me understand, in broken German, what had happened to 20,000 officers of the Polish army. They were out there somewhere, finished with, shot dead.

There was also a little 15-year-old boy, a Pole, who was a favourite with the *Kapo*. This little beast used to show off, teasing some of the hungry and sick, parading in front of them, while eating thickly buttered bread. Early one evening, I was very sick; I could not bend my knees any more. With all my strength, I climbed into my bunk, and I heard the boy say: 'Leon is kaput. Tomorrow in the crematorium.' I fell asleep but the next morning my temperature had gone and I was once again a begging barber.

One day, I left my bunk to answer nature's call. I had felt sick and emptied the contents of my stomach into the pail. I slowly walked back to my bed and tried to get to sleep. I was letting my tongue go around in my mouth and I suddenly felt that my dental plate with one or two teeth was missing. I sat up, thinking it must have fallen out of my mouth onto the blanket. I could not see it. I looked under the hay cushion but it wasn't there either. I looked over my bunk onto the floor but there was no sign of my precious dental plate. I could not be without a plate in my mouth. I would not be able to speak properly, I would lisp, and the men would make fun of me. Also, I needed to be well presented for when I went home.

I lay back thinking, retracing where I had been the last few hours: here in my bunk and when I had left it to visit the pail. Well, I could not find it in my bunk so it must be near the pail. I had been sick, perhaps it had fallen out of my mouth, onto the floor.

I climbed down, walked over to the nearly full pails. There was nothing on the floor. I got a hold of the pail and carried it to the lavatories just outside, which were only to be used by prominent prisoners and staff. Luck was with me, no one was in there. I took the pail and very slowly emptied the contents, so that only some thicker dirt was at the bottom. I held onto hope of finding my dental plate. I was busy when the door opened and the head doctor of the ward came in. He looked amazed and asked me what I was doing there. I told him. His face altered, he looked sickly, mumbled something and made a sharp turn to the door. Once again, I was alone.

I had nearly come to the very bottom of the pail and there, before my eyes, lay the much wanted plate. I picked it out with my fingers, cleaned the pail with water, put it back in its place and soaked my hands and dental plate in a large bowl of disinfected water, until I dare place it back in my mouth. I found my bunk and promptly fell asleep.

As the new much neglected arrivals came into the ward, they had to be cleaned up, so a shave and hair clip was the order of the day. The same happened to those fit enough to leave. One of my Dutch comrades had turned up – Mr Danzig, 'the Violinist' who played while I sang at Birkenau. I shaved him before he had to leave the hospital. He was very weak and almost cried. He asked what I thought was going to happen to him but I could not answer. I did not see him again. Nor did I ever see the tall, well-built Frenchman, who stood up next to his bunk, half-alive, hanging on. He had a hole in his back as large as my fist and pus was dripping out, as if it were yellow blood.

My friend Heinrich, who had shared the secret of the gold coin I found in Birkenau, also arrived on our ward. He had been a tall, strong man but he was now a crawling skeleton, a *Muselmann*. He was no more than skin covering his ribs, arms and legs, and his eyes looked into nowhere. He was a starving man.

Time went on. One evening while I was in my bunk, I heard from some Dutch prisoners that a well-known boxer from Rotterdam was a *Kapo* in one of the barracks. He was my old acquaintance, Leen Sanders. He used to be a champion boxer, fighting in nearly every country in Europe. I could hardly believe my ears. I had known all his family, his parents, sister, brothers. I had joined his brother's training school for boxers. I had seen him come and go from Westerbork and now he was here, and a *Kapo*.

I asked one of the young men wandering around the ward if he would like to take a letter to a certain *Kapo*, in exchange for a little of my food. He agreed, after making sure that I wasn't joking. I wrote a few lines on a piece of paper I found, explained who I was, and asked Leen Sanders to help me with something to eat. I did not want to beg for food – there was still some pride left in me – but what did pride matter? It was a case of live or die. I hoped for the best.

It was quite a long time before the young man returned. The evening was drawing in before he came back to my bunk. He held a cap in his hand in which were about half-a-dozen potatoes in their jackets. I was very pleased to have made contact with my old friend. I handed two potatoes to my comrade and ate the extra food.

Hunger was the main pain, and some were not so lucky as I. If you were caught trying to steal bread from others, the *Kapos* could punish you in whichever way they wanted. One young men was caught stealing bread and was made to stand up on a seat in front of the ward, with a piece of cardboard hanging around his neck, on which was written: 'I am a bread thief.' He had to keep on calling out 'I am a bread thief, but I will not do it again' over and over.

One day the SS and hospital staff got hold of a mound of black olives. Bowls filled with the salty edibles were handed to us in our bunks. Many could not eat a lot of them, but I did. I collected hundreds of olives in my bowl, and even borrowed more bowls to collect the discarded food. At one time, I had three bowls of black olives. I took the stone out of each one – work which took hours – then I cut them into little pieces and fed on them all day long for about three days.

There were always thieves about. I had my bread stolen at least a dozen times but only once did I pinch from my fellow prisoners. I was lying in my bunk, with wounds to my heels and arm, feeling feverish, thirsty and hungry – very hungry. Next to me was a Polish Jew: we were trying to talk German and Yiddish to one another.

We turned to the subject of food and, from underneath his blanket, he produced a cap full of potatoes, with a tiny one on the top. I asked him to lend me a few, but he was not having any of it. I promised I would give him potatoes from my next ration – I would even have given him my pieces of sausage the next morning. But no, he wanted my ration of bread. But bread was gold dust to us in the camp. I lay there thinking, feeling the raging pain in my stomach. I was in real need of something to eat and I could not get anything until the following morning.

It was late evening and the lights were low, so I tried to get some sleep. The ward was silent, only the regular breathing of the men could be heard. I found my hand very slowly moving from under my blanket into the bunk of my Polish comrade. I had made a promise to myself that I would hand him back a potato from my next ration. I was going to try and borrow that tiny little potato from the top of the pile. If I was caught, it would mean the end of me. Stealing from comrades meant discharge and who knows what else. At last my hand had found the cap under the blanket, my fingers searched for the little one, took it, and slowly I moved my hand from under the blanket, into my bunk. My mouth met it and I ate the little potato, as quickly as I could. The young man was puzzled when I handed him two potatoes from my ration a few days later.

It was the only time that I ever pinched anything directly from my comrades. While unloading food for the kitchen – cabbage or beetroot – I would take some and eat it raw whenever I had the chance. I found some lettuce leaves in a dustbin: a prominent prisoner had thrown them away because they were too big. I picked them out, cleaned them carefully and ate them. Delicious! I needed all the vitamins I could find if I were to pull through and get home again. I could not stop other men stealing from me. I tried to hold over the little piece of bread which I earned by shaving the prisoners but somehow it was gone before I ate it. It was best to eat all that you received the same day.

Shaving and clipping prisoners' hair gave me a little extra, but there was never enough. The whole idea of the SS was to bring men out here, make them work and starve them until death took over. We were just like weeds. We had to be destroyed. I was one of these weeds. Among all the thousands of men, I felt lonely. It was a question of everybody for himself, the weak to go sooner than the strong ones. But go we had to, all of us.

6 Auschwitz – Camp Life

At last the day arrived when I was to leave hospital and face the life of fear outside. Inside the hospital, you had a certain kind of protection. You did not work and you could do little wrong, so beating and bullying was not heard of. I had to register again with my commando, unloading trains full of cement, bricks and stones. I felt weak, and I got a few days leave to stay in camp. It meant you could lay in your bed to rest several hours a day, but, if there were too many of these cases in the camp, the SS would give the order to empty the beds. You were not fit for work, so you had a date with the gas chamber.

On a sunny day, I was working with a group of men in the commando, unloading parts of wooden buildings and carrying them to a building site. I stopped for a few minutes and noticed others peering into the distance. A long row of men was slowly marching in our direction, closer and closer they came. Some could hardly walk, others had bandaged heads. Some were carrying cardboard boxes of food – non-Jews, who were allowed to receive parcels from their homes in Poland. I saw my comrade who occupied the bunk beneath me in the barrack. His head was bandaged and he had been in hospital sometime. He had stayed in the barrack for a rest period and now he was marching with the other men towards the gas chambers. I would never see him again. There must have been about 1,500 of these men, passing us, marching into the distance. How terrible it must have been, for some of them realised that they were going to die. What was the use of struggling any further. When hope is gone, everything is gone.

The days came and went, every day the same miserable routine. At about 5 o'clock in the morning, the bell would sound and a loud voice would shout: 'Raus, raus!' – 'Up, up, out of the beds!' We would scramble out, slip on our trousers and wooden-soled boots, rush down the stone stairs into the wash room, hold our heads and faces under the taps and let the cold water clean our half-asleep faces. Others waited behind for their turn, so you had to hurry. If not, the *Kapo* would see to it that you could not mess about any more.

One morning, I was waiting near a man who was cleaning his head and face and was taking rather a long time for my liking, so I tapped him on the back and told him to get a move on. The man turned around and his soapy face looked at me: 'Who the hell …?' I had actually touched a *Kapo* and told him to get a move on: I was certain of a good hiding if he got hold of me. I quickly went out of the room, walked down the corridor, and then turned back again and placed myself in another queue. I had been lucky once again, for the bully had been using soap, which had got in his face and eyes before he could have a go at me. My little walk had saved the situation.

After the quick wash, we rushed up the stairs for now our bunks had to be made up. Everybody saw to his own mattress: it had to be shaken up, and the blanket tucked in such a way that everything looked just straight and proper. If there seemed a dent in the finished product, a bit of beating or bullying would follow. The SS would then come into the barracks for a quick inspection.

One morning I was awake earlier than usual. I had to visit the lavatory and, on my way down, I noticed the table in the corner covered with our rations of bread for the day. There was one whole black loaf cut into four pieces, not the same size. The large pieces went to the barrack's favourites, the smaller pieces to non-favourites like me. I also noticed the first piece of bread was a large quarter. The first in the queue will receive a big ration, I thought. No one was about so I rushed downstairs, washed myself and got back to my bunk. I only had to make up my mattress and I would be first in the queue. For once, I would get the first large piece of grub. I finished my bed making. Everybody was about now, either washing or making up their bunks. I was already number one in the queue – this would be a real treat. I always got a small piece of bread or a thin ration of soup, and I was always hungry. Oh, that lovely bread.

And then it happened. A loud bullying voice was calling out my number: '98288. Der Englander.' I could not think what they wanted me for. I had my eyes on the first ration on the table. I shouted: 'Here I am, here!' The bully said: 'Come here! Have you made your bed up?' 'Yes,' I answered, 'I did.' Then the face and finger of the shouting man drew near me. Getting hold of the back of my neck he dragged me from my place and towards my bunk. He slapped my face and pointed his finger towards my bunk. It was upheaval, like a Sunday morning tussle with my young son in bed. I got on with the job of straightening it up for the second time. I felt like falling through the ground, full of indignity. Someone had messed up my bunk and so I had lost my place in the queue. My chance of an extra bite of bread was gone. But what could I do? I was now last in the queue and when I took hold of my ration the bully laughed at me. He had been too clever for me, and one of his favourite mates now had the larger portion of bread.

The blankets we had to cover us at night were full of fleas. I used to watch them jump about on my arms and suck my skin. A blue light was always on during the night but it did not hinder the fleas. I used to wet my thumb and finger and get hold of the little monsters and kill them. Even at my work during the day, I used to feel the fleas biting my legs. I used to stand still, get hold of the turn-up on my trousers and suddenly turn it over. There would be a dozen or so jumping away.

I felt very unhappy in the barrack I was in. The *Kapo* was a disagreeable, short-tempered brute, who used to pester us whenever he could. Once or twice a week we had to strip off our clothes and walk out of the barrack into the open and enter a smaller one which was rigged out with hot and cold showers. Most of us had no soap and so we just stood there jumping up and down beneath the hot and cold water, enjoying it. But I would have liked to have had a bar of soap. Sometimes I found a very thin piece, probably left over by a prominent bully.

One Sunday afternoon, after working during the morning we were resting on our bunks – some sleeping, some dreaming, others just whispering to mates. Then the command was heard: 'Undress for bathing!' Everybody stripped as usual and marched out into the open. We got into the bathroom and took our places under the showers. It made us feel cleaner and, in about ten minutes, the command was given: 'Outside everybody, into your barrack.' Off we went, the same long row of running men, wet and steaming. Then we dried ourselves as best we could – only a few of us had towels. I dried myself with my jacket, dressed and, as it was a Sunday and there was little work to do, lay on my bunk.

After about 15 minutes, the *Kapo* commanded again: 'Undress for bathing!' We thought it funny. Had he forgotten that he told us the same about an hour ago? So, naturally, we stayed on our bunks, but the command was given again: 'UNDRESS FOR BATHING!' Then the staff made us get up and strip again and off we went; the long row of naked men, in their boots, marching into the bath house; and under the showers; then back to the barracks, past the laughing face of the mad *Kapo*. He had disturbed our Sunday rest. He must have been fed up, so he played his game with us. Still, water did not harm us.

It was unpleasant to wake up during the night, because the lavatories were two flights downstairs. Many a time I found myself half asleep, standing in the lavatories and then rushed back to my bunk, and just fell asleep again, tired out.

One evening when we returned to our barrack from work, we were all locked in and told that we had a quarter of an hour to have a good think about which one of us had wetted in a corner during the night, instead of going to the lavatory. If the one responsible came forward, all would be well. If not, all 500 of us would be punished.

We stood there between our bunks, talking and wondering. No one was going to take the blame so, when the *Kapo* opened the doors, he got no satisfaction. He then ordered men with sticks in their hands to take up positions and said: 'Get down, bend your knees, and keep on moving up and down with your arms outstretched. Keep moving until I come again.' There we were, rows and rows of men, moving up and down with our bended knees: if you stopped because you were out of breath or your legs ached, you were hit on the head with a stick by watching staff. This went on and on until I could not move any longer. My legs had given out – some of the men fell forward, on top of one another.

At last the doors opened and the *Kapo* looked in. He told us he was satisfied now and that we could go outside. It was another of the crazy things in the concentration camps.

The men in camp had to be shaved and have their hair clipped every Saturday and Sunday morning. I helped shave the prisoners with a razor given to me by the barracks' chief barber. When the last man was shaved, we had to hand in our tools. If I had a razor, I could earn a little extra soup or piece of bread from shaving the prominent prisoners in my barrack so I asked the chief barber for his permission. Sometimes he refused – it depended on what kind of mood he was in. One Sunday, I was late handing back my razor. I had done a lot of shaving and I thought I might be able to earn something extra by attending to some prominent prisoners, so I kept it, hoping the chief barber would not mind. I found my bunk and got to sleep as usual.

The following morning, a *Kapo* took us into a little wooden hut and demanded we empty our pockets. He wanted to find some tobacco or something he might find useful. I emptied my pockets, without showing him the razor. I did not have much to show, some pieces of string and a few nails. Then he felt my pockets and found the razor. I was done for. It was an offence to have a weapon of any kind.

He asked who was my *Kapo*. When I told him, he whistled. He did not like him. He marched me back to the barracks and the razor was shown. My *Kapo* was arguing with the other bully, then he took me outside the hut and asked me how and why I had the razor. I told him the truth and then it happened. The brute punched me in the face and kept on hitting me. Down I went, I got up, he started again. I could not and dare not hit out. Time and again I fell to the ground. I was bleeding from the nose when, at last, the bully let me go. I had to be careful of my *Kapo* now. He would have it in for me and I would have to try and keep out of his way.

The week passed and it was Sunday again. I was shaving the prisoners and the *Kapo* who had beaten me up stood watching. He walked over and told me quietly to take a razor out with me, for he wanted a shave in his hut. I told him he had beaten me up because I had the razor last week and now he wanted me to do the same. Nevertheless, I thought it best to do as he said, so the following day I shaved the mad man in his hut. A week before, he had given me a good hiding and now he did not mind.

Selection took place at regular intervals: the weak men were sorted out from the strong and so it happened that some were sent away from Auschwitz to work in other camps. Twice my number was taken to be sent elsewhere but I did not like the idea very much. The administration clerk of my block was quite a nice fellow. I told him that I would like to stay on, to help shave and cut the hair of prisoners. There were, of course, several ex-barbers to each barrack, so there was no shortage of help. But, somehow, this clerk withheld my card and I stayed on. After all, I did not know whether it would be better to go or stay. I took a chance.

Life went on at Auschwitz. Up at 5 o'clock, quick wash, dress, make your bed. Then queue for bread and margarine, sometimes a thin slice of sausage and some imitation coffee. Then you made your way to a large square and found your commando positions. We joined up in rows of five and waited for the command to march off to work. We marched on to the road and through the iron gate. Above it was a sign saying 'Arbeit Macht Frei', translated to mean 'Labour makes free'. At first I thought, if you work hard enough perhaps they set you free. But it really meant: 'Work yourself to death, then you'll be free.'

We were often told to sing while we marched. I did not know any of the German songs they were singing. I listened and thought how comical it all was. But when the melody was one that fitted some English words, I uttered them somehow, especially Roll Out the Barrel. I would often tread on the heels of the men in front of me – my feet were so sore in my awkward boots.

Usually we unloaded the trucks with their cargoes of bricks, cement, iron rails and pipes. One-, two- or even three-hundred men with their shoulders and hands on the sides and back of the trucks, pushing the train further up the line. This kind of slave work was always accompanied by bullying, shouting, hitting and kicking. If I find the *Kapo* who kicked me in the side, while I was pushing the train, I would do the same to him. If I had the chance to get hold of the *Kapo* who made me unload a fully laden truck of piping, piece by piece, because he did not like Jews, while he was cursing me, calling me all kinds of names, I would do the same to him.

Unloading bricks was a common task. Some men jumped into the truck and handed the bricks down to waiting carriers. It meant four, six or eight bricks on top of your shoulder, walk a distance, and place them on a heap, then walk back to the truck and repeat, on and on, sometimes for the whole day. I had the knack of placing my four bricks so that the centre two broke in half. The top of my fingers were often raw from handling them. Most of the time, movement was slow; a row of thin, miserable looking men was moving towards death. Whenever we could, we slowed down, for we wanted our energy to last as long as possible. Some of the men had been doctors in civilian life and they told me to spare the heart as much as possible, for on these rations of food and ill treatment you could not survive long.

I found a group of Dutch men together talking about politics. Some of them I knew from Westerbork and there was Bram Springer, a fairly strong fellow who worked in the gardens at Auschwitz. It was not hard work but Springer did not get home again.

One sunny day when work was done, we marched back into the camp square to find a row of gallows neatly laid out. I counted 12 and 12 little stools. I thought it was a show, to try and frighten us. We got into position for roll-call – my place was like a ringside seat for the gallows. There were thousands of us, hungry and tired, craving for our beds. When the counting was over, no command was given to break up. A heavy silence come over us. There, coming towards us were 12 of our men, well-built, clean-shaven, hair clipped, smiles on their faces. They passed me and I saw their broad backs. A command was heard and the men stopped in front of the gallows. Could this be true? This was no scare: it was a real execution, happening before my eyes. The men got onto their wooden blocks and a noose was placed around each of their necks. I could not believe it. I made myself look at every movement, so I remembered these strong men who were going to be hanged.

I heard a command and saw the slim figure of an SS officer in a smart uniform with silver braid. He held a sheet of paper in his hands and was reading from it. He said the 12 men were to be hanged, as a warning to us all. Three of them had tried to escape so the other nine were to be hanged along with them, to teach us a lesson. Then the camp *Kapo* went along the row of men. He tightened the noose of the first man and kicked the stool from under him. The man's hands were tied behind his back and his body started to turn sideways. Then it was the turn of the next one and so on until it was the turn of the seventh. The noose had not been placed correctly around his neck and when the *Kapo* kicked away the wooden stool, his body dropped but the man was fighting death. He turned from side to side, his face was red and blue and his tongue came out of his mouth. The *Kapo* grabbed the twitching body and pulled it downwards. The noose tightened and the man died.

When the 12 bodies came to rest, there was silence. The many thousands of us watching were stunned. We had to watch, we could not do otherwise. At the sides of the gallows were two machine guns with SS soldiers behind at the ready to shoot if necessary. One wrong move and hundreds of us would be killed. After a while, the bodies were cut down and placed in a heap, like old clothes. They were placed on a trolley and wheeled away. We were told to break up and get to our blocks. We were served our evening soup as usual but no one spoke. I will always remember what I witnessed that day.

On Sundays the same square was used for entertainment. Twice I watched a powerfully built prisoner, all muscle, bend iron into all kinds of shapes, and lift six or eight men by balancing a strip of iron on his head. His name was Samson. If you were caught at work doing nothing, your number was taken down. When you arrived back into camp the same evening, you were called out and the gentlemen SS officers would have their sport with you. One method of punishment was to make you roll over and over like a dog, jump up, lie down, jump up, lie down, run up, run down a slope of ground, crawl on your elbows, to and fro, just like a circus act.

Samson was often told to hand out punishment with a stick. Samson could not refuse for it would have been done to him. One night, an SS officer handed him a stick and ordered him to give a prisoner 30 lashes. The victim had been caught napping at work and now he was to receive his punishment. He was held onto a wooden horse, his pants taken down and lashes given him while the SS officer counted. These punishments often left the prisoner with such terrible wounds, he could not recover. The gas chamber was the only answer.

After the war, I met Samson. I read in the *Jewish Choronicle* that he was to give a demonstration in the Trades Hall in Edmonton. It was quite a surprise for me to read about him in the paper. He was in London to demonstrate his strength and collect funds for Israel. I hurried to the Trades Hall. Many people were already there, moving about and waiting. I looked around and spotted Samson seated between two ladies. He looked different now, dressed in a suit; his face somewhat blown up, hair growing. I stood in front of him and told him that he was the strong man who demonstrated his strength at the roll-call square in Auschwitz. He looked up at me, pulled my jacket downwards and said to me: 'Wasn't I good for the boys.' I did not answer. I straightened up and left him after the ladies asked me something about him and the camps. I did not answer them either.

I stayed on and watched his act with the iron bending: the men hanging on to the end of the strip of iron did not move according to commands and Samson lost his temper and shouted out, telling them what he wanted them to do. I left the hall after a while. I had my thoughts about Samson.

One day, at roll-call, I felt drowsy and sleepy. I did not feel good and my body kept weaving backwards and forwards. I saw an SS officer to my left and closed my eyes, hoping he would not notice me. My mate behind told me to stand up properly but I was falling backwards and could not keep my eyes open. Suddenly I felt a pain between the legs and my eyes shot open. I looked into the face of the SS officer who had kneed me in the groin. I immediately stood to attention, but he just looked at me like I was a bit of dirt and walked away. Once again, I was saved. I tried to get back into the hospital for a while. I wasn't feeling too good, low in spirits and miserable. The doctors could not find a valid reason for letting me in.

The day arrived that I was to leave Auschwitz. I had been there for about six months. On 15 September 1943, some of us were told to stay behind after evening roll-call. We had to take off our clothes and wait for an SS officer to inspect us. And I was one of 200 men to be sent to another camp.

We were told to get onto a lorry with a military jeep full of SS officers following us. They held a machine gun at the ready, should any of us try to escape. I had to leave my mates behind and look towards the next camp.

7 Monowitz

After less than an hour, we arrived at the new camp. It was called Monowitz and held about 10,000 prisoners, mostly Jews. It was known for hard labour, terrible winters and the usual harsh concentration camp life. We were stripped, and had to visit the shower block. The camp was on a much smaller scale than Auschwitz, but the pattern was the same.

That evening, we did not receive any food. We felt hungry but had to wait until the next morning when we were registered and moved to different barracks. I was to join a small commando. The *Kapo* was not a bad chap, and the work was the same – fetching and carrying as before – but the food rations were smaller than at Auschwitz. Hunger was getting to me more than ever. I once again offered my services as a barber, clipping and shaving prisoners every weekend, for everybody had to look clean and tidy when they marched out of the camp for labour.

The gong sounded at 4.30 in the morning and we jumped out of our bunks; on with our trousers, bits of socks or rags, or just naked feet, into boots or clogs, with your jacket under your arm. You dare not enter the washroom with a jacket on. You washed the top of your body with cold water, from taps fixed above a round basin, about six or eight men bending over with you, letting the water run over their heads, shoulders and face. Quick, not too slow, with hundreds waiting their turn. You didn't hang about, for someone would get a hold of you and push you away. But clean and fresh you must look even without soap.

Then it was out of the washroom and back to the barracks. You had your jacket on by now and your boots were blackened with a black, oily liquid. It made your hands dirty and sticky if you did not use it carefully, but the front of the boots looked shiny and black. You looked presentable, standing there in the queue for your ration of bread and imitation coffee. As it was your turn to take hold of your ration, one of the staff called out your number so that any double rations mistake was out of the question. With your ration of bread, you either stood near your bunk, or ate on the edge of the lower one – but very carefully, for you had made up the bunk so it looked presentable should there be an inspection.

When you had eaten your morning rations, you went outside. Often there was a little time to spare, so I went around to another barracks where I could find the Dutch prisoners huddling together, talking about the war and the chances of getting home again. I remember Nico Gosselaar, a radio mechanic from Wassenaar. He was one of the most sensible men of the group. He knew all the answers and assured us of many things. I met Nico several times after liberation. The last time I met him he was in hospital with heart trouble. Soon after I visited, he passed away.

The gong was sounded and everybody hastened to the square. We found our commandos and an SS officer would come along to inspect us. Off went all our caps or berets and each one of us stood stiff to attention, looking straight ahead. If the counting of the prisoners was correct, a command was given to relax. You could then whisper to your mates, as long as the SS officer didn't see you. When the whole camp had been accounted for, it was nearly six in the morning. If it was winter, the snow and cold winds played games with you. You longed to get walking, for the cold went right through your body. If it was summer, the air was fresh, the sun was coming up, and perhaps you felt a little more contented with your fate.

I watched the commandos walk out of the gate until it was our turn to do the same. We marched to the sound of the camp orchestra, with uncovered, clean-shaven heads, hands and arms pressed against our legs, looking straight ahead. Many a curse was in our minds as we passed the SS officer, looking strong in a green uniform with silver braid, like God Almighty. We looked like the walking dead, all of us thin, like planks of wood, with large bony heads, cheek bones and chins sticking out.

Arriving at the work site, the commandos separated; each had their own place, some inside, some out in the open fields. My work took me outside, unloading train loads of building materials, mostly cement. How many bricks must I have carried in my life? How many sacks of cement? Sometimes I dug the ground for pipe laying. We worked slowly, very slowly if there was no one to watch us. One of us would take position where he could spot an SS officer or a *Kapo* in the distance. He would give us a sign, call out 'Arbeit' ('Work') and all of us would get busy shovelling until the danger passed.

In the summer, the sun was hot and we were cursed with thirst. In the winter, the cold, snow and frost destroyed us. Painful, cold feet and hands, not much clothing, not much food, only a little hope left of getting out of this life.

One warm and sunny Saturday afternoon, I was standing near an open window shaving one of my mates. I had been away from Holland nearly a year now and all of a sudden I heard my name being called from the outside. The sound of the voice was familiar; I looked up and answered the greeting. It was my old friend Jacques de Wolf. I stepped outside for a minute, having finished my customer. We shook hands and asked about one thing and another. Then a man next to my friend began to speak in Dutch and he said the following words, which I will never forget.

'Greenman, you are one of the most unfortunate fellows.' I asked why? He told me he had worked in the registration department at Westerbork. Soon after the train had left on the morning my wife and child and I were sent away, my name was being paged all around the Westerbork camp. On opening the morning mail, a letter was found telling the authorities that Leon Greenman and family had to be interned as British subjects. Kurt Schlesinger had not opened the mail until after the train had left Westerbork. He could have said 'yes' if he had opened his mail.

Nonetheless, I was pleased to have found my friend Jacques and some other new arrivals from Rotterdam. There was Jaap Theeboom, his son Joop, and Jupy Kattenburg. All of us mixed and met after work was done. I remember one Sunday I walked into the barrack, Jacques showed me a photograph of his family and I said: 'You have something to go back home for, something to stay alive for.' His wife was a non-Jewess and was left unmolested.

Time went on. I shared my extra food with Jacques and the others many a time. Jacques was caught one day in an air bombardment from the Allies. It was a Sunday, the working parties were out of camp, and he was one of the men caught in the raid. He spent some time in the camp hospital: one of his eyes was all

colours. Jupy Kattenburg was also wounded. I wandered alone
for a while, the rest of my friends being in the hospital.

Work varied, but it was always heavy. I seemed to be picked
to heave bags of cement. One or two prisoners would jump into
the truck while the others below stood with their backs ready to
receive the load. I was always too short so the bags would fall on
top of me, instead of being placed. I was afraid of this kind of
work. One of our Hungarian mates took two sacks on his back –
he was a show off. If the *Kapo* had noticed, he would have made
us all carry the double weight. We soon made the strongman
understand his stupidity.

After my day's work was done, I got my usual ration of soup
and then went to the barrack singing. Soon I was known as 'the
English Singer'. I sang anything I could remember, although
my voice had lost a lot of its quality. But it was still appreciated
and I felt content to go to my bunk with half-a-dozen pints of soup
or several slices of stale bread in my balloon-sized belly. The sur-
plus of my earned soups, I saved until morning and handed it to
some of my Dutch friends who could do with the extras.

My singing was not always appreciated. Sometimes I opened
the door of a barrack, asked the chief if I could sing to the men,
and the bully would take hold of my bowl and sling it onto the
road. I always tried the next barrack, remembering to stay away
from this one. One evening, I was invited to sing in a barrack.
Halfway through my second number, 'Ave Maria', a hefty *Kapo*
walked over to me and kicked me between the legs. He was a
boxer in life, in camp they called him 'the Boxing Master of
Breslauw'. He was a bad beast and I stayed out of his way.

Luckily for us, not all the *Kapos* were bad. I remember one who
gave me food quite often, without me having to sing for it. One
afternoon, he asked me to stand up and sing to a gathering of
perhaps 1,000 men, all seated in a field in a circle around me.
Later on that evening, I collected my soup.

The *Kapo* of Barrack 14 was a German, aged about 50. He was
very anti-Nazi, probably a communist. The first time I knocked
at the door of his barrack, he listened, gave me bread and soup,
and said to his staff: 'This is a fine singer and a singer must eat
well to be able to sing well. Every evening he comes here to sing,

give the chap a ration of soup. And on Christmas Eve, I want him to come and sing to all of us.'

Every evening I went along: sometimes I sang, sometimes it was not necessary. But on one occasion, the decent German (if he was German) called me into his little room. His staff were there as well, one of whom spoke some English. I was commanded to sing the national anthem, 'God Save The King'.

I alerted them to the fact that about 100 yards from the barrack, an SS guard was on duty and, in the quiet of the evening, he would probably hear me. But they did not care and I hardly minded as long as I got my food. So, standing on a chair, I sang, somewhat quietly, the national anthem, and some of the men hummed with me. All went well: they applauded and gave me pieces of bread and some soup. And when I left, there was no need to try another barrack the same night, for I had enough food to still my hunger. Some time later, the chief of Barrack 14 was sent elsewhere, and so ended my 'ration for sure' at this barrack.

First in Auschwitz and later in Monowitz, or 'the Buna' as it was known, I saw men in khaki uniforms moving about in the distance. I heard some of my mates mention that they were English prisoners of war. I began to wander away from my group, towards the British prisoners. These were my people and I wanted to talk to them about what was going on in the camps. My foreman shouted and asked me what I was doing walking away from the group before orders were given. I told him that I was English and that my real mates were over there. The group laughed at me and asked whether I wanted to be shot. It was an offence to talk or mix with prisoners of war, punishable by shooting. I stayed and listened; I bided my time.

One day, by chance, I was asked by my *Kapo* to try to get some cigarettes from the Tommies. From then on, I mixed with the POWs as often as I could. They gave me cigarettes, slices of bread and soup. I talked to them about the Germans and the life our prisoners were leading, always hoping somebody could get me out of this hell. Some of the soldiers were kind, others just indifferent. Some offered me an escape route to their camp and perhaps to liberty, but I declined. How could I? – A little thin fellow, with short clipped hair, a number on my arm, looking and smelling of concentration camp life. I'd have to stick it out.

I've forgotten most of the names of the soldiers. I wish I could meet some of them or perhaps they would remember me, but the chances are slim. One name has always stuck in my mind. Sergeant Aldridge with whom I spoke for some time, explaining who I was and my need to get out of Auschwitz and Monowitz. Mr Aldridge mentioned that he came from Woolwich, London. All at once we were spotted by an SS boss, which resulted in me being severely beaten by my *Kapo*. This happened in the morning. If the beating had taken place in the evening, after roll-call, I think I would not now be talking about Sergeant Aldridge.

There was the soldier from a place near Brighton who gave me a bar of chocolate, Cadbury's or Nestlé. I broke it into pieces and offered some to my mates but none of them dared take any. It was an offence to take anything from a POW and they were too scared of the beating they'd receive if the *Kapos* found out. Perhaps I forgot; perhaps I was too hungry to let this chance go by; perhaps it was a pleasant feeling to receive a piece of English chocolate from an Englishman. I ate the chocolate and enjoyed it. I could not care less about anything else.

Later on, some of us worked inside the POW building and there was often an extra piece of bread or a portion of soup left over for me. One afternoon, we were unloading a train of bricks when I noticed some POWs having their tea. They were frying eggs. I had not seen or tasted an egg for such a long time. I was quite near to the soldiers but dared not speak to them as we were being watched.

We kept an eye on the eating men. How hungry we were! Then I noticed that a small piece of egg had fallen to the ground, just too far away for me to grab it unnoticed. I felt like a beggar, pleading for food. I did not want the soldiers to think I was begging, so I kept my eye on the spot where the little piece of egg had fallen, hoping that the soldiers would not step on it and bury it in the sand.

I made up my mind to get the piece of fried egg. It was as big as the nail of my thumb. My mates knew what I was after and kept watch on me. When the soldiers finished their tea, they moved off, and, in no time at all, I jumped over the bricks between me and the piece of egg, picked it up carefully, took it to my mates and cut it into four. Those nearest to me had a tiny piece of egg and it was delicious.

I mixed with the POWs whenever I could and often I could not be found at my place of work. The cigarettes I received from the British POWs I exchanged in camp for soup. There were always men in the staff of the barracks who cleaned out the remains of the soup containers, and so had plenty to buy cigarettes with. Three British cigarettes for a large bowl of soup. But I had to hand over some cigarettes to my *Kapo*, from time to time. He wasn't a bad man, he never beat you, but then it was a small commando he was leading. He used to tell us to wash our feet with plenty of cold water at night before going to sleep. It would prevent you catching cold or flu, he said.

The way I was always around the British soldiers must have given cause for complaint from my building site chief. So, one bad day, I found myself transferred out of his commando into another. This was one of the hardest commandos known in camp – the cable laying commando – consisting of 400–500 men who had to drag and lay telephone cables throughout the camp.

The *Kapo* was a Dutchman; *Kapo* Job they used to call him. But beneath him were several other *Kapos* – they were bad, making you work like a horse and bullying you all the time. The men had to lay the cable in a dugout. This way, by pulling it along between their spread legs, holding it with their hands, and shifting it inch-by-inch, sometimes two or even three cables were laid a day. It was very hard for my morale – I became ill with scurvy, my body covered with hundreds of pimples and itching all the time.

There were hundreds of us unhappy men, all scratching ourselves. So we were isolated and placed in a barrack separated from the others. We were never allowed outside, nor could we wash ourselves and we had to smear our bodies with a kind of black ointment. We scratched until sleep overtook us and that didn't always happen.

I remember a Dutch friend of mine, Theo Cohen. He was about 23, had nearly completed his diploma to become a doctor of medicine when the Boche had picked him and his family in Holland. He and I had been good pals, and now he had arrived in this scurvy barrack. I saw him deteriorate day by day, until he died. Once again, my guardian angel was with me and I got better and left the cursed place and got back to my cable commando.

I developed piles and was suffering with them now. One morning my Dutch friend Jo de Groot who slept in a bunk next to me and with whom I shared a lot of time, took me by the arm. He said that I had no need to march out to work that wintry morning, for, as the commandos were marching out to work, the men who felt sick and unable to go could report to the camp hospital for treatment. And so, my friend Jo walked with me to the doctor at a spot on the square. I felt too much in pain to talk, so Jo did it for me, telling the doctor that I could not walk very well. I was allowed into the hospital. I stayed about five days, my ailment soon passed and the little rest had done me good. Then I was sent out of hospital into the open, cold reality once again.

I was put to work to dig the ground and, not far from me, I saw a couple of women digging the ground. They seemed much stronger than me, it was the way they handled the shovels. It had been a long time since I had spoken to a woman – I had seen some on the building sites, carrying bricks, but I had not talked to them. It was forbidden.

One of the women nearest to me nodded and I nodded back. We came nearer and, as I could not talk her language – I guessed she was Polish or Russian – I made her understand that I felt weak and could not dig as well as she could. She smiled. I spoke a few words of German and learned that she was a prisoner of the Nazis. I was always troubled by a runny nose because of the cold weather, and I used to wipe my wet nose on the sleeves of my coat or jacket. She must have noticed it, and my embarrassment. For the next day Rosa, that was her name, handed me a small blue-spotted handkerchief. I did not see Rosa again, for my work with the commando was elsewhere. And so a friend was lost again. Not that the sight or the nearness of a woman made me feel different. I did not even notice that I was missing the company of women.

In camp some of the *Kapos* received tickets every now and then. With the tickets they were permitted to visit the barracks with women in it. This barrack stood alone from any other and was surrounded by barbed wire. I noticed SS soldiers going in and out. Sometimes, when we stood on the square for roll-call, some of my mates mentioned that the non-Jewish men like these

Kapos were allowed to seek the company of the women, and asked if I ever wanted to follow suit. My answer was that I never felt that way – it could be my own wife in there, forced to satisfy these men.

Again I sought the protection of the hospital. I had burned the sides of my legs and developed large sore patches. I showed the doctor and was allowed to stay for about a week. It was warm in there, one could lie in bed all day, no work. But then again there wasn't a lot of food, just the regular rations, and there was no chance for me to earn anything extra. They had their own barbers, and so the only thing to be thankful for was not being beaten up or bullied. So long as you were not a nuisance, you were out of the wintry weather for a while. Polish winters could be terribly hard.

Better for the rest, I rejoined my commando and during the weekends I helped shave the prisoners, which brought me a little extra food. I was also singing from barracks to barracks, receiving extra soup. I was again mastering hunger.

Life did not vary much from day to day, but sometimes the Nazis put on something special for us to think about, such as hanging prisoners who had tried to run away from the camp. After a day's hard labour, 10,000 or more of us marched into camp walked into the square and took up our positions for roll-call. My place was front row of my barrack position and I faced a gallows, where two nooses were hanging empty, waiting for their victims.

The orchestra played marching music right until the last men had entered camp. Then, after roll-call, we all stood and waited, no running away into the barracks for the little food we were given. We saw SS men taking up positions, machine guns in hand. They had us covered in case some of us wanted to start something, not that we could. We had no guns, we knew we were beaten. We wanted to stop the hanging but we had to do as they wanted.

The unfortunate men to be hanged were marched from a prison barrack; they mounted the gallows. A noose was placed around each neck by some of our own men, who were ordered to do so. Then an SS officer read something from a paper. The handle was brought down and the body dropped. Its feet partly inside the trap, the body slowly turned around and back again –

the hands tied behind the back could not support the agonies of a hanging man.

I remember the two men, just before the final drop. They shouted out loud – 'Let us live, we will work', 'I want to live' – but it did not help them. Or the four men hanged, and just before the drop, they shouted: 'Let us hope that we will be the last ones to hang.' Or the young Frenchman: he could not have been older than 17 or 18, the expression on his face showed he did not understand that he was about to be hanged. It was September 1944.

When the special spectacle was over, we were commanded to make our way into the barrack, passing the bodies. Once in the barracks, hunger took over. Here it was everyone for himself, look out for beatings. Often we were kept waiting for our rations – first we had to undress and look for lice in our shirts. If you found one, the whole barracks had to strip and go bathing; everybody received clean shirts; then you could queue for your soup, which was sometimes warm by now. I got wise to the fact that the soup in the metal containers was not stirred around a lot. It meant that the thick part stayed at the bottom and only the thin was handed out, thus the first few dozen in the queue received nothing but thin liquid. The ones further up the queue received somewhat thicker soup. I often tried to fix my place so that I would get some of the thicker brew. Often it happened as I wished, but often it happened that, just as I was holding out my bowl, the staff would halt and take a fresh container, with the result that I received something like warm water.

Selections were held regularly. The weak men were sorted out from the strong (or still fit-looking) men and within a few days the weak would be sent to the gas chambers. It was mostly done on Sunday afternoons. No one was allowed outside the barracks, doors were shut and guarded, windows closed. The waiting was long, this terrible suspense of thinking: 'Who would it be this time?' You made a mental picture of yourself, with firm buttocks, and muscular arms and legs. Some of the men knew they were doomed. They could not work any more. Others were sure they would be all right until the next time.

Then we heard the talk – they are coming – and the door opened. The camp doctor, a Pole, came in with another and they

18. One of these huts is 'Loods 24' in Rotterdam, through which some 12,000 Rotterdam Jews passed on their way to camps.

19. Kurt Schlesinger, head of the administration department at Westerbork camp, where Dutch Jews had to assemble before being deported to concentration camps. If Schlesinger had opened his morning post before the train containing Leon and his family left Westerbork, he would have found documents relating to the Greenmans' British nationality. Schlesinger later escaped to the US, where he lived until his death.

20. The entrance to Auschwitz II – Birkenau. The trains arrived on the right-hand track. Abandoned luggage lies strewn on the other tracks (Państwowe Muzeum Auschwitz-Birkenau).

21. New arrivals at Birkenau being divided by the SS (Państwowe Muzeum Auschwitz-Birkenau).

22. Professor Horst Schumann, who experimented on Leon's body at Auschwitz. He was arrested in 1966 in Ghana, and his case came up in 1970. However, in 1971 he was set free on account of his 'illness'.

Model 119

No. 7 1 2

Register V . *folio* . *n°.* 9 6 6·

In de registers van de burgerlijke stand van Rotterdam is ingeschreven het overlijden van

Greenman, Barnett, geboren te Rotterdam 17 Maart 1940
in de omgeving van Oświęcim(Polen)
overleden op 1 Februari 1943 . oud

gehuwd met

gehuwd geweest met

zoon/~~dochter~~ van Greenman, Leon en van Dam, Esther
Akte van overl. ingeschreven   Leges *f* 0.50.
18 Apr. 1951
                        Ontvangen. 16 November 1951 .

Model 119

No. 7 1 1

Register V . *folio* . *n°.* 965

In de registers van de burgerlijke stand van Rotterdam is ingeschreven het overlijden van

van am, Esther, geboren 23 Febr. 1910 te Rotterdam
in de omgeving van Oświęcim(Polen)
overleden op 1 Februari 1943 . oud
laatstelijk
gehuwd met Greenman, Leon.

gehuwd geweest met

zoon/dochter van

Akte van overl. ingeschreven   Leges *f* 0.50.
18 Apr. 1951   Ontvangen. 16 November 1951 .

23. Else and Barney Greenman's death certificates, which state that they died 'in the region of Auschwitz' on 1 February 1943.

Barber of Buchenwald

HE CAME FROM FOREST GATE

From ANNE MATHESON: Buchenwald, Wednesday

A s I was leaving the Buchenwald concentration camp, I met Leon Greenman, an Englishman from Glenpark-road, Forest Gate. He was thin and hollow-eyed, but in good spirits, for Leon had his passport to home and freedom.

He had been liberated from Buchenwald, and was waiting an airplane to fly him home.

Leon has lived in this foul concentration camp for more than four months, and before that he lived at Birkenau, on the Polish border, where he submitted to almost unbelievably cruel tortures.

He is alive only because a Polish doctor hid him in a hospital when his feet were frost-bitten after forced marches and, while being herded in trucks in a long journey from the Polish frontier, he collapsed.

Leon, who was a barber in peacetime, said: "When the Russians were advancing we were brought to Buchenwald. I was living in Holland with my wife, who is Dutch, when war broke out.

Too outspoken

"I was a little too outspoken against the Nazis, and one night they picked me up with my wife to a camp in the north of Holland.

"From there I was taken to Birkenau, where I saw all the horrors of thousands of prisoners being killed in gas chambers.

"At this camp I saw my wife and son for the last time. I suppose they were killed. I remember kissing my little boy good-bye from a carriage window, then waving to my wife, and we were taken to different camps."

Leon told me that he lived on potato peelings, was forced to carry hundredweight cement kegs all day.

24. *Evening Standard* interview, April 1945.

25. Leon in the British Red Cross hospital in France, recovering from an operation on his foot. With him are his French friends, Gaston and Suzanne Pron.

RED CROSS ENQUIRY/MESSAGE

Stamp of issuing Red Cross: *PARIS* (stamp)

JH/

ENQUIRER
DEMANDEUR

Name/Nom .... Mr. GREENMAN,
First Names/Prénoms ...... Leo
Date of Birth/Date de Naissance ....
Nationality/Nationalité .... British
Address/Adresse ...... Hertford British Hospital, Paris, - via BRC, Paris.
Original Home Address (in the case of a Displaced Person)/Domicile dans son propre pays :

Relationship of Enquirer to Addressee/Degré de parenté du demandeur avec personne recherchée
.... Brother

The enquirer desires news of the Addressee and asks that the following message should be transmitted to him :
Le demandeur voudrait des nouvelles de la personne recherchée et désirerait lui transmettre le message suivant :
...... Liberated from Buchenwald, - recovering in British Hospital,
Paris. Want news from you all, hope you are well.
No news of wife and son, deported in 1943.

Date ...... 17 May, 1945.

ADDRESSEE
DESTINATAIRE

Name/Nom .... Miss GREENMAN,
First Names/Prénoms ...... Kitty
Date of Birth/Date de Naissance ....   Place of Birth/Lieu de Naissance ....
Nationality/Nationalité ..... British
Single — married — widow(er) — divorced (Delete all irrelevant matter).
Célibataire — marié(e) — veuf(ve) — divorcé(e) (Barrez les mots qui ne servent pas).
Profession/Profession ....
Last known address/Dernière adresse connue :
...... 97 Jubilee Street,
London, E.1.

The Addressee's reply to be written overleaf (not more than 25 words).
La réponse du destinataire (25 mots au maximum) peut être écrite au verso.

S.&D Ltd.—21817

F.R.59/1937

26. Telegram from Leon to his sister Kitty in London, searching for information.

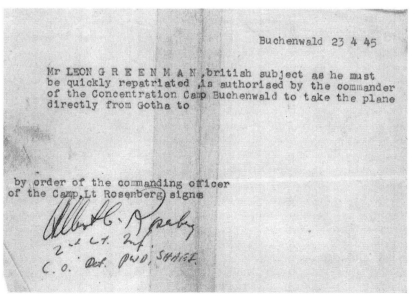

Buchenwald 23 4 45

Mr LEON G R E E N M A N, british subject as he must
be quickly repatriated is authorised by the commander
of the Concentration Camp Buchenwald to take the plane
directly from Gotha to

by order of the commanding officer
of the Camp, Lt Rosenberg) signé

2nd Lt. Inf.
C.O. Det. PWD, SHAEF.

27. Instructions from the US Commander of Buchenwald camp for Leon, as a British subject, to be repatriated.

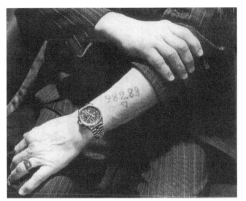

28. Leon shows the number that will stay with him for the rest of his life, 98288.

30. Leon Borstrock, No. 98281, the only other survivor of the 50 men chosen from Leon's transport.

29. Leen Sanders, European boxing champion, who survived Auschwitz. He died in Rotterdam in the early 1990s.

31. Leon as 'Leon Mauré' – his stage name during his years as a performer after the war.

32. Leon behind his market stall.

33. Leon as guide on one of the Anti-Nazi League's organised trips to Auschwitz, September 1996. Leon is an active participant in the ANL's work against racism.

34. Leon receives his OBE from the Queen, 24 February 1998.

seated themselves near the window so that light would fall on the naked men as they paraded before them.

'Everybody undress!' In a few moments we stood naked between our bunks and followed the long row of men, who came before the doctors in turn. Turn your back, stand for a few seconds, and your fate was decided. Some were too thin for further use: their index cards were handed to someone – if your card stayed in the box, you were spared, at least for a while.

Barrack after barrack was subjected to the same routine: many knew they had two days or less to live. They would say goodbye to us one morning and we would never see them again. Jaap Theeboom, my acquaintance from Rotterdam, although a strong tough man at home when working on the ships, was thin and weak in camp and was identified to be sent to the gas chambers. But somehow some of his mates managed to lose his card for a while.

On and on went this life, every day the same pattern, only now and then something for the worse, hardly anything for the better. Seeing the British POWs in their military uniforms usually made me happier, especially when I could get near enough to talk to them.

However, one POW made me feel particularly miserable and low in spirits. One winter afternoon, snow was falling and about a dozen of us were pushing a large iron pipe on a wheel barrow. On and on we went, pushing, dragging, over the snow-covered rough ground. I looked around and saw a khaki uniform moving way back in the field, a soldier making his way towards the wooden urinal. I asked my foreman if I could go to the lavatory – it was a welcome stop for the men and a welcome journey for me, to speak to one of my own.

I entered the hut, approached the British POW and started to talk to him in English. He looked at me and asked: 'Who are you?' I told him I was an Englishman, born in London; caught by the Boche in Holland; sent to Auschwitz with my wife and child. I said that it did me good to talk to the POWs whenever I could. He cut in, saying: 'While you and I are suffering our loss of freedom, your mates, the Jews in London, are doing a good trade on the black market.' I was surprised and said: 'My brothers are in the army. Not all Jews are working the black market.' He shrugged his shoulders and went out of the hut.

I felt lonelier now than ever. One of my own had talked like the Nazis. I rejoined my commando and did a lot of thinking about what the soldier had said. Now I wasn't sure whether I was right in looking for the company of Tommies: perhaps there were others who talked like that.

The winters were terrible for us ill-clad men. I had trousers, a jacket and a top interlocked under my jacket. Long coats were handed out to us, some civilian, others blue-and-white-stripe camp issue. The coats had half a square foot of cloth cut from the back near the shoulders and a red-and-white-striped piece of cloth inserted so that you were noticeable from a distance. If you were seen running away, a guard could take better aim at you.

I was wearing a civilian coat and a nice one at that, in good condition and nothing cut out of the back. I wore it for a few short days before I was told to leave it with the barrack tailor to be 'put right'. I went to work for three days without a coat, in the cold and wind, so they could stitch on my stripes.

When the gloves were given out, I did not get any in my barrack. One early morning I made my way to the barrack where gloves were sometimes handed out either to the hospital patients or to various barracks.

It must have been about 5 o'clock and no-one was at the barrack. I waited and waited. Then a man came along; he saw me at the door and asked me what I was doing there. I asked him to let me have some gloves because I had not received any. Instead of giving me gloves, he handed out a short but damn good hiding and I went away, feeling more unhappy for this incident. I worked without gloves throughout the winter.

Bit by bit I was losing my grip on things, and at times I was in very low spirits. In the barrack where I lived, I used to help shave and cut the hair of the inmates, every Saturday late afternoon, and Sunday morning. For this I received a ration of soup. But I also served some of the more prominent prisoners, such as the *Kapos* or foremen and for this I was paid with pieces of bread or soup. The chief barber of the barrack handed out the razors. I found my razor none too sharp, it caused lots of agony. I made my way into the *Kapos* room, where the chief barber was shaving one of the *Kapos*. I stood there for a moment, then I approached and asked for another razor. I can still see the *Kapo* under the razor of my chief barber, move the man aside, and leap from his chair. He landed a terrible kick aimed at the lower part of my body: I managed to step backwards, and so the kick lost a lot of its power when it landed on me, but I made haste to get out of the madman's way.

Later on I got my sharp razor. Another incident which could have meant the end for me happened on a warm day. We barbers were told by the barrack chief to keep a certain space of the room only for shaving the men: no one was allowed there unless he was to have his hair clipped or be shaved. I had to strop my razor and I walked over to the strap. I somehow touched the feet of a young *Kapo*, who stood there with the upper part of his body naked – sunbrowned, muscled shoulders and chest, his hands at his sides. He shouted at me, I had by accident touched his toes. He demanded an apology. I told him, he had no right to be in this space of the barrack, and that he was in *my* way. He lifted up his arm and meant to bring his hand down on me: I felt miles away from the spot where I was standing, all I knew was I was right in what I had said, according to the chief of the barrack. I felt my razor in my hand, it was opened. At the same time as the hand was going to land on me, I said in a loud whisper: 'If you dare touch me, I'll cut you with my razor, so true as I am standing here before you!' His hand stayed in the air, he had noticed my posture and my face, and by God, I wasn't kidding. I would have let him have it, because I was nowhere in a concentration camp. At that moment all I sensed was that someone was trying to get at me. The muscleman stepped back, and disappeared into the room of *Kapos*. I expected to hear more about it, but I did not. I kept out of his sight whenever I could. I had gone too far maybe but I had been lucky.

Another incident in my barber's career will stick with me. In one barrack even the chief of staff – a Polish Jew, always neatly dressed – was among my 'clients' sometimes. That particular week the bunks in the barrack were being painted by one of our men, also a Polish Jew, and he too was among my lot of men for a close shave. Not just the once over, no, I somehow gave him a good, clean shave, and we seemed pals all right.

During the Sunday afternoon, I was almost finished with my job. I noticed that my bunk had been painted. I knew I had a piece of bread underneath my straw pillow. Wanting to make sure that it was still there, I went to my bunk, took off my boots and climbed onto the second bunk. I felt for the bread, yes, it was still there. All of a sudden, the painter shouted at me. 'Get off the bunk! I have painted it, get off!' I answered while getting down: 'It is all right, I haven't my boots on, and I did not touch the wood. I wanted to make sure of my ration of bread.' I thought the incident over. But, no, I was called for by the chief of staff, and asked why I had got onto the bunk, when it was forbidden to do so. I was surprised and wanted to tell him why, when his hands and fists came down on me, again and again. I was bleeding from my lip, and my eye was hurting, I was left alone, everybody around was surprised and some told me to be quiet, for I was letting my feelings get the better of me. I looked at the painter standing there, laughing at me. I went to him and said: 'You are a dirty Jew. It is a dirty trick to put another Jew onto me for such a trifling reason.' He made his way to his friend, the chief of staff, and came back with him. He in turn asked me why I had called the other a dirty Jew, and, as I tried to explain, he started punching and hitting me all over the place. As he left me on the floor, some of the men helped me up, and told me to be wise and say nothing more about it, that the painter was a nasty fellow. I did not say any more about this incomprehensible incident. But I did not shave the painter again; he went to one of the other barbers. And the other gentleman did not seat himself in my chair. Soon I left this barrack for another.

Life became more and more miserable for me; I was probably reaching the beginning of the end. Often, while I was digging, I use to let my mind wonder. 'Why was I here?' Apart from the awful mistakes as to my nationality, why was I here? Oh God! Why? Answer me.' And then I imagined a voice say: 'Because you're a Jew and the Jews are a bad lot.' Yes! I was here because I was born a Jew, and my forefather was a Jew, and so on. That was a crime. But surely not all of us were bad people. My little son was not a bad chap. My wife wasn't a nasty somebody. I did not have to pay for my bad things in life in this terrible way. Why feel like that about it, Leon? Why?

Sometimes I could see a train travelling along. It could be a train loaded with people on the way to the camps and death. I wished I could do something for these poor people. Suppose I could find the power to stop that train, by magic, open the door, and let the people off. Stop the SS from lifting their arms, just let them stand dead still, like models. Nothing to stop me from using the power given to me, using the same power to stop the war, everybody go home, become better citizens, a better world. 'STOP DREAMING, Leon.' I would watch the train passing me, and until the last truck turned the corner.

But sometimes it would be a train with empty trucks, or some of the trucks loaded with shot-down aeroplanes, partly burned tanks, guns and other war material, all coming back from the Russian front. Good for you, Russians. Hit them, hit them hard and wherever you can. The war was turning slowly against the enemy. It did us good to see the broken up war material coming back from the front. Our men would look and say to each other: 'That is good, but it will be too late for us.'

I used to look at every truck as it came along and passed me by. Trains for the Netherlands had 'N.S.' on their trucks. Holland. HOLLAND! Off went my beret in salute. My mates use to say: 'Oh, Englishman, what are you doing? Are you mad?' But I knew better: Holland was a sad memory to me and, all the same, I went into a dream again. Suppose I could get passed the SS guard, get underneath one of those Dutch trucks; hide until it reached Holland again, let myself drop somewhere in Holland and I would be almost home again, and then get away across the sea; to England. Away from this lousy, terrible, unhappy life. Wake up! Leon! It can't be done.

How my feelings were quite different, bitter and hateful, when I saw the trains coming from the German side, loaded with fresh material, newly painted tanks, planes, guns: all going to the Russian front, killing, KILLING more and more. Why did the Boche not stop this lost battle, or was he really winning this struggle for existence? No, the Jerry would never win this war, it could not be, it must not be. Did I not make a promise, that I would come back home again? So the battle was lost to the Germans? If it would only hurry up, and come soon. Oh God, don't let the end come too late for me and my mates.

Everyday the same, again and again. Up at 4.30 in the morning, for me 4 o'clock. I wanted to be first in the wash house, first out of the tumult, the pushing and scrambling. First back into the barracks to make up my bunk and then queue for my ration of ersatz tea and piece of bread. Then off to the Dutch comrades. Listen to the news they had to tell: the news of invasions, liberation, and so on. I did not ever say much, I was only a little, thin miserable-feeling chap, shivering with cold, stamping my feet. How we all got close together to keep the wind away, and all the time we knew to tell better news than the others. Until all of a sudden there was the sound of the bell: everybody scrambled off to roll-call, and commandos. Then marching out to work while the orchestra was playing. Walk head high, look straight in front of you; out of the corners of my eyes I could see the SS officers watching us pass by. And then the shout of the *Kapo*, as he went by the SS, calling out our commando number, and how many men he had with him. It all had to be the same in the evening when we marched back into the camp.

Arriving at the camp site, go get your shovel and pick axes, and then on with the work, whatever it was: digging large holes in the ground, for what? I never really knew what we were digging for. I did not care, just let your arms and hands and legs move, so that the cold would not get the better of you.

Sometimes you asked permission to pull out to go to the lavatories: a wooden hut with a board in which there was one or more round holes. You sat there, taking more time than necessary. But it did not matter a lot, as long as time went by. Only never overdo it: you could never tell, even your own mates might call it a liberty.

I'll never forget the day when I went as usual to my 'wooden hut of rest' for a while. I had taken the usual route behind the SS guardhouse when, all of a sudden, I heard a voice shouting out. I stopped and looked around and saw to my horror the SS guard, calling me. (I had never had anything to do with an SS guard for I knew they were fanatics.) I walked back to the guard, who had come down from his watchtower, gun over his shoulder, and was waiting for me at the bottom step. I halted in front of him, not knowing what he wanted from me. He asked me where I was going. When I told him, standing stiff to attention, his hand came down in my face, and he said: 'Why are you walking behind the watchtower? Why not in front, so that I can see who and what is walking?' I felt insulted and said: 'I always take the footpath

86

behind the SS guard, and have done so for a long time, several times a day.' I did not know that the SS man was a fresh guard who had his own views on the matter. I had never found any trouble with the other guards. He told me that, as long as he was there to guard us, he would see that everybody passed in front of him, and that I had to tell my mates about it. I was told to go. I was lucky, but the feeling of having had the hand of the Boche in my face was a big insult to me. After all, I was a British subject!

Some of the SS guards were mad. I remember the morning when one of our chaps, a Hungarian, arrived at the site of work. He jumped down a hollow of the railway line, as he had seen some cigarette ends lying there. The SS guard came rushing over, shouting to our foreman that he was going to shoot the man, for he had walked off the ground over a border, which he was supposed not to do. Our foreman quickly argued with the guard, and pointed out that what the man had done was only natural, picking up some cigarette ends to smoke, and that it was the foreman's responsibility if the man had left the queue for a few minutes. It would not happen again. The SS guard answered that a next time he would shoot directly anyone that passed the border-line. When our foreman questioned if the soldier did not believe in God, the SS man answered: 'Herr Schwatz the chief SS commander. He is my God.'

Uberstormbahnfuhrer Schwartz was a much feared SS officer in the camp. He was the one who made some of us strip in the middle of the fields when on our way to work in the winter time, to see if we had anything with us that was forbidden. I was lucky to escape one day from his hands. I had been shaving the inmates during the Sunday, and during a short interval I wandered off into the room of the *Kapos*, where my chief barber was working. I had a bundle of white cheese underneath my jacket, having received this from a foreman I had shaven. All of a sudden the door flew open, and there stood the big bulky figure in SS uniform, his big, black, beady eyes looking into the room. This was Herr Schwartz, the big chief of the camp. A voice shouted 'ATTENTION!' and everybody stood where he was and stopped whatever he was doing. I stood to attention and, as he stepped into the room, he looked here, looked there and then he noticed me, little Leon. I had a large chest, and, of course, the cheese packed underneath my jacket was very noticeable. Herr Schwartz walked over to me, grabbed my chest and bundle into his hand and demanded: 'What have you there?' I answered: 'Some white cheese, Sir.' He looked straight at me and said: 'He! What!' I thought I had to explain again and had no time to think what might happen, but he let go of me, made for the door and disappeared. That was the end of the incident. I think of Schwartz whenever I eat white cheese! He was to be executed in Auschwitz later on.

The morale among our own mates wasn't always happy. Many a time I was called names, because I seemed to be treading on the heels of the person in front of me whenever we were shovelling sand or gravel. I went fast to keep my blood circulating, or as an exercise, but the others said I was overdoing it. Or again, if I was working too slowly, I was cursed; or when my shovel had touched the man's hand in front of me and injured his little finger, a few minutes later, the same was done to me. We even went to bash one another with our shovels, nearly.

During the summer months at the camp, on some Sunday afternoons, boxing matches took place. Among the prisoners were several champs, one in particular – Young Perez – the French bantam weight champion of the world. We slept in the same bunk for a considerable time, and I often awoke to find the arm of Perez across my face or chest. I pushed the arm away, which would waken him, and he would start grumbling, and then, realising that it was me, he used to say: 'Ah, Anglais.' He and I were good friends; he had fought Jackie Brown in England before the war, and on the whole he had pleasant memories of the English, Perez did not come back from the camps. He had bad feet, and I suppose he was left on the fields or roads during the withdrawal from the Russians, when the Boche was evacuating the camps.

There was a Dutchman, Kleerenkooper was his name. We both went to present ourselves to the *Kapo* who organised the boxing matches and asked whether we could be matched. When he saw us, he laughed and told us to go and forget about it. We must have looked thin and unfit: a pity really, for the winner received a whole loaf of bread, or even two.

Boxing was one of my favourite sports. I did quite a bit of training before the war at one of Bram Sanders gymnasiums: I had put a lot of heart into it, just to keep fit. Bram was the brother of Leen Sanders, the Dutch champion of whom I wrote earlier on. My friend Bram did not come back from the camps, neither did the other Jewish boys I used to train with.

On a Sunday afternoon, I wandered out of my barrack onto the large square ground, where in the far-off corner a boxing ring had been erected, and boxing was in full swing. I noticed that lots of men were around the ringside, and I could not see anything of the boxing until I found myself standing on one side where there were no more than two *Kapos* watching. I did not ask myself why there were so few people at this side of the ring! I was pleased that I could see all that was going on without having to stretch my neck.

Suddenly I felt a heavy hand come down on my face. I looked up at where it had come from, and stared into the face of a tall *Kapo*, who had come quietly next to me. I was still wondering why, and what I had done wrong again now. When he asked: 'What are you doing here, you swine, don't you know that this side of the ring is forbidden for prisoners to watch. Don't you understand the gentlemen behind you have this clear view for watching?' All this while he was pushing me away. I looked behind me and there, believe it or not, about a dozen or so SS officers in their full party uniform, with silver stripes here and there, were the spectators at this side of the boxing ring. Unknown to me, but all the same true, I had been standing with my back towards them for a while, which was quite out of order.

I made off as quickly as I could, feeling insulted because of the smack in my face which had come so abruptly, and I felt robbed of a good afternoon's entertainment. Later on I saw the funny side of the incident: my backside had been on view to the SS men!

On another occasion, a theatrical piece was being performed by more of the prisoners. I had left it too late, but with a little effort I found myself inside the barrack. It was quite dark in there, and a full house. As I was looking for a seat, I felt a fist come right into my face, and my nose started to bleed. I was pushed outside the door. That was enough for me: I went on my way. It wasn't worthwhile getting a beating for trying to watch a piece of entertainment.

Another time, the word went around the camp that the chief *Kapo* wanted some singers for a concert. A Dutchman, Pennesick, and I went along to the *Kapo*. On hearing us, he shouted at me and kicked me outside the barrack. I did not care, I tried and tried, and if luck did not come my way, well, I let luck alone.

This same camp *Kapo* – a well-built German, about 45 years old, the fright of the camp – could give a damn good hiding. One day, he marched between 60 and 80 sick men into a lavatory, and locked us up. I was among these prisoners. We felt too miserable to march out to work that day and so we were locked up, instead of getting a doctor's examination. The *Kapo* told us we would get no food until the evening.

There we were, sitting next to one another on the wooden lids of the lavatories, a stone building with accommodation for about 12 men. Time went by and then we heard the camp gong go; it was lunch time for the prisoners in camp, such as those in the camp hospital, and the staff of each barrack. We felt hungry, for if we had been at work we would have received our portion of soup. Hungry men can do things: the first one of us peered through the window, opened it, looked left, then right and heaved himself up, and through the window, out into the ground and off towards his barrack, where he would receive a portion of soup, perhaps two or more portions. Soon the second and third man followed and, within a short time, almost all of the men had left the lavatories that way. Now Leon picked up courage, and I looked left and then right, to see if the way was clear; I heaved myself up, and leaned outside the window. Oh dear! it would mean quite a drop for me, for I was so short but, hunger or no hunger, I made the jump, and, as I picked myself up, saw in the distance the camp *Kapo* coming towards the lavatories. I called to the man at the window, who was going to follow me, to get hold of my hand and pull me inside again, as the *Kapo* was in view. Luckily he grabbed me as I jumped up, and pulled me inside. There only about nine of us were seated on the wooden seats. We saw the half-figure of the *Kapo* in front of the window; he peeped inside, saw that it was almost empty and went into a frenzy. Shouting at us, asking where the men had gone, claiming that he would get them later on, he disappeared. I tried to imagine what he would do to the men, if he ever got hold of them.

Then at last I tried again to leave the sickening place. I entered a barrack and the staff handed me a ration of soup. Then I made my way back to the lavatories and waited until camp roll-call. This was usually at about 3.30 in the afternoon. Half of the men had come back into the hut and when the *Kapo* unlocked the door he told us that we had to wait on the field after roll-call because he wanted to speak to us. But, as roll-call ended and some of the chaps stayed on, I noticed that they received some kicking up the behind and I did not feel like waiting for this, so I wandered off to my barrack, taking a chance that he would not recognise me again.

Yet another time I came into contact with this ill-tempered man. I had been singing in one of the barracks, and had just received my pay, a ration of soup. The air raid alarm went; the whole camp went into darkness; and everybody had to be in their barracks. But I was just leaving a barrack, trying to walk quickly alone, while holding the bowl with precious, hot soup in my hands. Then I ran into that *Kapo*: he shone his torch into my face, and started to shout: 'Back into your barrack, you swine.' With that he kicked me in the behind, making me stumble. But I held onto the bowl of soup, and started to run into the dark; at last into my barrack, where everything was also in darkness, I found my bunk, climbed up to the top, which was my place for sleep, and I did myself good with the thick soup.

Air raids and bombs falling around the camp made some of the bullies tremble. One fellow I knew – he wasn't a pleasant kind of chap – he lay there almost crying for his mother. To me, the air raids were music. It meant that at last the allies had found our camps. I did not mind finding death by a bomb from my own folk, if it had to be.

One afternoon, I was with a working party of Hungarians: we had been constructing a very deep trench for a water main, it had taken us a few weeks of digging, and building wooden walls to stop the earth from coming down upon us. There was an air raid alarm: everybody for himself, out of the trench, away. That was the command given by our foreman. I had climbed to the top, everybody was already yards away, when the youngest of our working party, a Hungarian about 16 years old, called out to me that he had left his package of bread below. He needed it badly. I knew bread was gold, to any of us. I stopped, and we turned back. I climbed down, found his packet of bread, climbed up again, and, on reaching the edge I handed him the bundle; then he made a run for it, leaving me to get out and over the top. I thought I'd never make it, as somehow I seemed too short to grab a hold of the wooden planks. That was a 'thank you' for me. I told him afterwards that he could go back himself, the next time.

I reached the open field, and bombs were dropping near a railway line, not far from us. I lay very close to the ground, pushing myself as if I wanted to get inside the earth. At the same time, I prayed aloud to God, not to let me die now because liberation wasn't far off. I felt like a worm in the ground – so little, and almost nothing.

The air raid over, we turned back to our work, and resumed as if nothing had happened. Returning to camp, when work was done, marching along, sometimes singing as commanded. Every evening I said to some of the men, again another day nearer to death or liberty. Nearing the camp gates, there were the SS officers, taking count of the returning men, the *Kapos* calling out the number of the commando, and the number of men; if all right, pass along. One evening we found a young man standing on a wheelbarrow, calling out: 'I'm here again, I'm here again.' If he stopped, an SS officer hit his feet or legs with a thin stick. The fellow had run away and had been brought back; for punishment and as an example to us, this show was put on.

Sometimes we had to carry four or more bricks from the fields, all the way back to the camp: they were needed for a new building. I dropped one of my bricks and received a kick from an SS guard. Never mind, press on Leon, press on; the enemy will get his punishment. Nonetheless I was not the same as when I first arrived; something was giving way in me. The whole idea of survival seemed so far away that I began to see the foolishness of the hope still in me. Perhaps it was my health, or the continuous feeling of fear around me. Be careful of this, or that. These spells did not do me much good and I found myself ill one morning. I did not march out to work, but went to the hospital and showed the doctor what I had discovered on my thighs: it was a red swelling. What was it? A huge abscess, or the result of a kick from a *Kapo*? It showed up in a lump as big as a fist. It made walking difficult, and it meant I couldn't work, so would it be the gas chambers for me?

8 In Hospital Again

And now I was in for it: *Phlegmone* was now developing on my thighs. It is the temperature going with this disease that makes you feel awfully ill. The doctors took a close look at the red patch. He then told me to wait; he was going to keep me in the hospital. I was pleased: it meant 'inside' for me, out of the cold.

After a shower, I was put into a bed on one of the wards. The following morning the doctor of this department of the hospital came around to have a quick look at us on the overcrowded ward: there were two men to a bunk, two bunks above one another. I shared mine with an Italian fellow; he told me he was a solicitor back home; he was a nice chap; a Jew; he was in good spirits, whenever we tried to converse he always smiled. His name was Leo. I had a high temperature and was perhaps sometimes snappy if I was not understood quickly enough but Leo understood, and gave me as much room as he could without letting his feet or legs touch my aching legs.

The doctor – Dr Sheiner or Sheineman, I think he was a Frenchman – came around to my bunk, and had a look at my thigh. He had with him a young Polish male nurse, who could speak a little English, because I was mumbling English and German together in my feverish condition. The doctor told me he could not yet operate because the swelling wasn't big enough and he ordered that cold wet compresses be placed on the red patch several times a day, after a few days it would be ripe for cutting.

The days that followed were uncomfortable ... I was asleep most of the time during the day. If I had to go to the lavatories I could hardly climb from my bunk, and almost crawled along the row of bunks up to the little wooden compartment at the end of the barrack. But sometimes I could not get out of my bunk, and had to call out for the bottle, and then one of the prisoner male nurses, or one of the recovering patients allowed to walk about the ward, would come along with the glass bottle, and take it away again to empty. If it happened in the night, it sometimes took a very long time to rouse somebody, and I was in agony.

The nights were uneasy for most of us. We were pestered by the many bugs, crawling from the wooden bunks onto your body and sucking your blood. You felt itchy all the time. Your sleep was disturbed, and you lay awake, semi-conscious, scratching yourself.

The day arrived when I had to be helped out of my bunk, by the friendly male nurse, the doctor's assistant, and taken to the little compartment for my operation. I was lying on the trolley stretcher and told to take a deep breath: a rubber cup was placed over my face, and I knew no more. I was too sick to care, or to be afraid of what might happen; perhaps I would not get home again. I just could not think very strongly about this any more.

As I came around again, I heard the doctor and assistant saying to me: 'That was a very interesting story, go on tell us more.' But I knew of nothing I could have talked about. I cried, I felt beaten, very sick and humiliated. The Boche had made me what I was, a nobody.

The bandages around my body were of white crepe paper, for there were no more cloth bandages. I was lifted into the arms of the nurse and taken to my bunk, where I had a good cry and fell asleep. The temperature was gaining on me. I was terribly thirsty and wanted to drink; water, please get me some water. But that was forbidden, to give water to the patients without the nurse or doctor's consent; but somebody did give me some from time to time.

I stopped eating and, as happens at times, the unexpected came along. One day the soup handed to me was a very thick one, with about five potatoes in it! But I did not feel hungry. I could not eat it and I held it in my hands, looking at it. It was of no use to me now. I did not want it. I looked up and stared into the eyes of my comrade Leo. I gave it to him and watched him eat it while I felt sleepy and went into a feverish dream.

The bandages had to be changed every other day and I was carried to the doctor because I could not walk or stand up straight. But the bandages, being of paper, tore away from my body when I turned from side to side in my sleep and I noticed the open wound. It was a large one and nothing was covering it.

The shirt I was wearing stuck more than once to the wound. But there was a shortage of bandages ...

The order was given that the ward be evacuated. All the patients had to be taken to other departments for a few days because this whole ward was going to be fumigated to get rid of the bugs. Already some men were sealing up the windows and other open spaces. The healthier patients who could walk were being directed to other parts of the hospital. The small batch of very sick men I was among remained in their bunks, waiting.

As I looked around me, I noticed on a table a few dozen cups, some empty, some partly filled with sweetened imitation coffee. We had been given some with our breakfast rations. I was thirsty; I asked somebody to hand me some of the remains of the drink; he did so, emptying the cups into one until it was nearly full; and I drank it all – the lovely, sweet, cold drink – but it did me no good.

It was my turn to be taken out of the ward. My friend the male nurse took me on his shoulders and carried me to a little room where I found several other sick men, all waiting to be distributed elsewhere. My friend spoke a few words of English with me and placed me on a chair, but I slipped to the ground and lay there. My body was not listening to me any more.

The doctor's assistant looked at me, and said in German to some others: 'The Englishman has had it, he is caput.' I knew what this meant: I was given up, I was on my way out. He picked me up, gave me a piggy back and, as he did so, my body could not hold nature's urge and I knew I had developed dysentery. I felt so ashamed; it was running from me. My friend was rushing me to another barrack for dysentery, from where plenty did not return.

My mind was still with me. I knew that the *Kapo* of this barrack was a good man who could speak English. Often (when I was still in good health!) I would have liked to have been in his ward for a while; he had a good name among the patients. And now I was in his department. I was handed over and put into a bunk where I lay speaking English. Somebody called out to the barrack leader that here was a Tommy. He came over to my bunk, asked me who I was, and if I were a Tommy. I answered that I was from London, and mentioned in a few words a few particulars.

He comforted me, and promised me that I would be with him until I was quite better. But within a few minutes fate had decided differently. I told him that I felt a terrible pain in my back and he promised to get his friend the doctor to see to me directly. I felt safe and, for the first time, a little happy: at last I had probably found a friend for keeps. Even if I was out of hospital, I need not go without food any longer for this man (a German prisoner!) was going to see to me and would hand me food when I needed it. I had heard all this before.

Not many minutes had passed, perhaps ten, when the doors opened and in came the barrack *Kapo* with a doctor. They walked up to my bunk; the doctor asked me where I had the pain and I pointed to my back. He gave instructions to get me out of the bunk, and had me placed sitting on a wooden seat. There I lifted up my shirt and he listened with his stethoscope to my back. I could hardly take a deep breath, I felt miserable again, and I heard the doctor say: 'pneumonia.' That was that.

I was immediately taken to yet another barrack. It was cheerio to my chances for a decent life: the dream was fading. I was put to bed, after having my number registered, and there I lay sleeping, waking, dreaming, calling out for water all the time. I was so thirsty that I handed my ration of bread to one of the men helping out in the ward if he gave me a cup of water: he did. And so I stopped eating, only drinking. But my rations were stopped because I wasn't in a state to eat my food: I had nothing to exchange for a drink of water.

I had a dream in which I saw nearly every member of the family, but I did not see my wife or child. When I woke up, I was in a kind of delirium. I was told to be quiet because I was disturbing the other men, all suffering from the same illness, and they were dying like flies.

A Frenchman had been listening to my loud-spoken dreams. He had become quite friendly to me, and, as I was lying near to him, I told him that I did not want to go on any longer. I told him my dream, and that I did not see my wife and child. His comment was to the effect: look here old chap, if you leave us, and suppose your wife and child get back to England, what is going to happen to them without you? This shook me up a bit, but it did the trick.

I was thankful to my French friend. He was a language translator in the film industry when he was still a free man. I think my friend (was his name Maurer?) did not get back to France again. I, however, started to pick up very slowly, eating my rations, and although I laid for days on end with my open wound unbandaged I pulled through again.

It was winter and I made up my mind to stay in this hospital as long as I could because I would not have lasted long once outside again. Every evening the male nurses took our temperature and noticed whether one or the other was getting better or getting worse. Several times I rubbed the thermometer against the blanket, causing the heat to register high; and so the nurse was taken in, reading my high temperature, marking my index card so. I was not the only one faking sickness.

One evening, while the nurse wasn't looking my way, I put my head under the blanket, took the thermometer out of my mouth and rubbed it just once against the blanket, and put it back in my mouth. When it was taken from my mouth and read, I was told to get out of the bunk. I thought I had had it this time. According to the thermometer I should have been a dead man, so high was the registration of my temperature! But another fellow had to come down from his bunk, for the same reason. There we sat, waiting, perhaps this would mean a dismissal, and out of the hospital I'd go.

Fortunately, the nurses had discovered that some of the thermometers were not operating correctly, and so we were ordered back to bed. I did not try this game again but I did use another trick. Every other morning the doctor used to call each man who could get out of his bunk, for close examination. If you were fit enough you had to leave the hospital the next day. So, just before it was my turn to climb down and stand before the doctor, I used to stick my head underneath the blankets, and make myself perspire. When I stood before the doctor, he noticed that I was warm and perspiring heavily, and he would send me back to bed.

These days in bed were not bad, especially if you had discovered a friendly patient to converse with. One day a man climbed into a bunk not far from mine: we were soon friends because he could speak English and many other languages. It was Serge Kaplan; he told me he had worked for the Philips firm in Eindhoven, Holland. How we used to talk about favourite foods! I mentioned I had a sister-in-law in London who was a good cook and made breadpudding. I had to explain to him what it was made of – bread and fruit. Here we were, lying in our bunks and talking about food. After liberation, I met Serge and his wife and lovely children; they lived in Hilversum, the Dutch radio town. We used to write letters to each other. He is mentioned in various books because of his knowledge of apparatus used to make medicines. Serge lives in Switzerland now.

I played my game with the doctor for about six weeks. Then one morning he called me down from my bunk, looked at me and said: 'Greenman, you must leave the hospital this afternoon; you may not stay here any longer.' I answered that I felt weak, but he told me that the SS doctor would be coming today or tomorrow to sort out those who were of no use, having been too long in the hospital, and that would mean the gas chamber. No patient was allowed to stay in the hospital longer than four weeks; after that a patient was considered incurable, only fit for the gas chamber. And I did not want to go to any chamber.

So, there I was, round about midday, in the cold open space. It was a habit and a camp rule that the weak men coming from the hospitals could join the kitchen staff for a bit, to get fit again; then out they went, into their own hard labour commandos. I was placed in the kitchen commando for about three weeks. It meant up at 4 o'clock, a march to the camp kitchen staff; there was the usual midday break; and back to your barrack at about six o'clock. The work was mostly helping to prepare the food for the prisoners and also for the SS company, the soldiers who were guarding the camp.

The potatoes for the SS had to be peeled in such a way that not one dirty spot was left on them; their greens had to be cleaned very thoroughly. Up to a dozen men did this kind of work. We had nothing to do with the actual cooking of the food, this was left to more professional men.

The food for prisoners was also prepared in this kitchen, but it did not matter that some dirt was left on the potatoes, or that the spinach was not free of sand. The hungry men would eat it in any case. How many turnips did I clean and cut? How much spinach did I wash? I had quite a knack in cutting some of the greens.

Many a potato disappeared into my stomach: we all did the same thing. We were always hungry and here was the place for me: lovely boiled potatoes, pick those that were just small enough to be popped into your mouth, no one looking, go on, quick another on, and yet another, but don't let the *Kapo* see you. The fellow who was responsible for the actual cooking of the vegetables – a Berliner called Siecky, I think – he was a decent young man, much liked; he was a Jew.

As it happened, and it always happened to me, the *Kapo* was a really bad-tempered man, and an anti-English man. Every time the Royal Air Force bombed a German town; he shouted it out to me and slapped my face, just as if I had done it. I used to say that the Germans were bombing English towns, etc. I tried to keep out of his sight as much as possible although he was always wandering in and out.

I had to try to keep my job as long as possible: the food was easy to come by. But the work was sometimes hard, such as carrying the empty metal containers from the various lorries, to be rinsed and cleaned in other departments. Two men to each metal container, these containers were too heavy for one man, especially for the weak ones.

One afternoon I was helping to unload the lorries, and waited for a second man to help me. All of a sudden I was dragged around and I received a terrible kick in the lower part of my body. I fell to the ground, I was in terrible pain, and my attacker was shouting at me; I ought to have carried the container by myself, not with another.

This Belgian–Polish Jew, a foreman in the washing department of the kitchen, had done this to me. Every one of the men around me was surprised. He had no reason to do this to me, since I was the responsibility of the other *Kapo*. Our foreman Siecky came rushing out of the kitchen, and asked what was going on. He picked me up, took me inside and shouted at the other man, that he should not have done this. But there it was: the harm had been done. I was soon sitting down again, peeling potatoes, after this disqualification.

One morning, I was in the lavatories which were a good way down the fields. I was there quite a while when there was a knocking on the door. Siecky was calling out: 'Greenman, where are you? It's roll-call, and everybody is waiting, come on, hurry up!' As a bullet, I rushed to the kitchen while tying my bit of string around my trousers, thinking at the same time, what was going to happen to me now? What would the *Kapo* do to me? What would the SS officer do, or say?

I entered the kitchen department and saw all the men, about two dozen, standing in line, waiting for the little Englishman. I saw their looks; they expected something to happen to me. I took up my position, the *Kapo* had seen me walk in. He came up to me and smacked my face just once. And then he called out: 'Ready for counting, Sir! ' The SS officer came in and counted us and it was back to work. I did not hear any more about it. I was lucky once again.

Well, I ought not to have eaten so much: I would not have needed to go to the lavatory in such a hurry. But, then again, food is lovely when you are hungry.

There was also the Sunday afternoon when, being Sunday, there wasn't much to eat in the camp, so I could do with the extra, even a raw cabbage, but I could not lay my hand on anything. I hung around the kitchen for a while, and when I saw young Perez, the world boxing champion who shared my bunk, asked him for the promised soup. In the kitchen were a few Greek men; I used to shave and clip their hair sometimes. Yes, Jackie the boxer and the other tall heavyweight. I'll always remember: young Perez handed me a bowl of the wonderful food, and I stood out of the way in a corner eating it, very slowly, blowing every spoonful, for it was very hot.

Then, a door opened and one of the kitchen *Kapos* came in. I heard him say that the whole camp was waiting for roll-call but one of the prisoners was missing, and everybody was speculating. He noticed me in the corner, eating my soup. He pointed to me and shouted: 'You are the missing prisoner, get out of here, you fool, hurry, they are waiting for you.' He took the bowl out of my hands, and pushed me through the door. I saw 10,000 men, lined up in order for roll-call. Dead silence was everywhere; they were waiting for me. I was the missing person. Now how am I going to get into my barrack position without fuss? The camp *Kapo*, the big bully, was pacing up and down the rows of men, and re-counting them. The many SS officers responsible for the correct total of prisoners were waiting patiently. And there was I, also waiting patiently for a chance to slip into my position without the raving *Kapo* spotting me.

I got my chance: all faces were turned away from me, and I rushed along. Lucky for me, my mates were standing nearest to my side, and I got to my place, and stood as if nothing had happened. Again the counting took place, and everything went all right; some of my barrack mates whispered to me: 'Luck was with you, Leon.'

Time went on; my stay at the kitchen was over, and I was given work in the potato cellar – a wooden shed, in which were stored potatoes, cabbages, turnips, and so on. I worked there with some half-dozen men, sorting out vegetables. Most of the time, when the *Kapo* wasn't there, we tried to get at the barrels of pickled beetroot, or the cabbages. I remember my pal Jo de Groot working with me; he liked beetroot, and, while I kept watch, he handed some to me, for he was nearest to the barrel.

The *Kapo* – Schiller was his name – was a German; sometimes he lashed out with feet and hands. His bunk was in my barrack but I mostly kept out of his way. During the early part of 1944, the weather began to be more kind to us, new transports of men arrived; one small consignment of Hungarians was put to work with us in the potato shed.

The men looked quite healthy and fit, they must only just have been picked up by the SS. The meal on one of those days was spinach soup: not very appetising, but I believed the vitamins in spinach would make me stay fit a little longer, and so I liked everything that was made of greens. The Hungarians did not care much for the meal: they left it standing on the low table before us. I was staring at the men, and wondering why they did not eat their food. I casually enquired if they liked the food, and whether they were going to eat it, or leave it. If the latter was the case, then perhaps I might have it? They made me understand that they cared not for the food and I was welcome to it. They walked away from the nine bowls filled with spinach soup.

I got hold of each bowl in turn, poured the juice away and ate the remains – a bowl of spinach filled to the rim. I thought I had eaten the best meal for a long time; anyhow a load of vitamins like that would add to my fitness.

On and on, day after day, loading, unloading lorries with potatoes, cabbages, turnips. I pinched a cabbage and ate it raw, bit by bit. It tasted wonderful. It was June 1944, I was in the kitchen sitting next to my friend, a Belgian diamond-cutter by trade. He spoke Dutch to me and told me a rumour that the invasion of France had begun, and that we could expect a big turning-point in the war.

I had been longing for the liberation. I said that, if I heard that the Allies were still in France in the following week, yes, then I would believe the rumour. My friend had heard it from someone else, who had heard it from someone else, and so on. The rumours sometimes affected our morale; all the previous ones were turning out to be false and hope was squashed.

The day arrived when I left the kitchen commando for good, and had to join up now with another hard labour commando: the digging and carrying, pulling and tugging had come my way again. I had to sing for my extra food again. Of one thing we were sure, the war was turning against the Boche. Many old SS guards were used to guard us; the younger men were being called away. There was a very young boy of about 15 or 16 years. He came quite close to us while we were digging the ground, almost on top of me, and he got talking with one or two of us prisoners. He told us that he had fought on the Russian front, killing many, and he seemed quite proud of it, the way he placed his hands around the leather straps which were holding his gun, and rifle.

I daresay, he would not hesitate one minute to shoot any of us, if he thought it necessary. An older SS guard, a man of about 45, was guarding us regularly, and he talked to us sometimes. I listened, I did not converse and others told me this older SS officer was quite afraid of the youngster, in case he gave him away for some reason or another.

I thought of how some of the SS were drifting towards us in conversation, but for me they could drop dead: if the war had gone their way, they would not be talking to us now. I remember during one afternoon, a very old SS guard was near me. He must have been nearly 70. He looked down at me as I was digging and shovelling the earth. He made a gesture to me that I need not work so hard at it. I stopped and looked at him, the old boy; was I pitying him? He told me that four sons had been killed in the war.

What could I do about that? It serves them right. But perhaps it was a bit hard for the old man and his wife. He was holding a pipe in his mouth, but had no tobacco to smoke: he made a gesture, no tobacco. I thought for a minute. I had found a piece of cigarette, I felt for it and I threw it up to him. He thanked me.

9 The Death March

It was January 1945. In cold, windy and dreary weather some of our men were digging large open spaces in the ground. They were supposed to be for gun placements. Was the Boche getting ready for a last stand? We could hear the Russian guns firing quite near now. We picked up rumours: the Russians were about two days away from our camp. Would they get here in time? What would happen to us?

Everybody could feel the tension; nobody knew anything; and all of us were guessing; laughing on the inside. It had taken a long, long time, but the end was very slowly coming into sight.

The order came to us not to go out to work any more. We had to stay in our barracks and prepare for a journey. We had to dress ourselves as best and as warm as we could, for the journey would be long and cold, and it was going to be on foot. I had only boots on my feet. At Auschwitz we halted a little while: again, I saw thousands of men dressed for a long journey. Monowitz was being evacuated. The Russian army was nearing Auschwitz and the Nazis were making their escape. Hitler had ordered that everybody had to leave the camps. No one was to be left behind for they could be a help to the Russians.

I was one of the Monowitz thousands who began the death march to Gleiwitz. It was to be a march of 90 kilometres in heavy snow; heavy snow falling from the sky, freezing weather. Stopping was not allowed. Those who could not make it and fell to the ground were shot. Those trying to escape across the snow-covered field were shot. The SS had no mercy for us. We were paying dearly for Hitler losing the war.

It was snowing. I was getting cold. Although the march warmed us, somehow the quick breathing in and out seemed to tire me and others. For a very short moment I saw my old friend Leen Sanders. He was also dressed and ready to get marching: we hoped to see each other after liberation, in Holland.

Commands were given, and once again we marched through Auschwitz onto the open road. Walking, marching, walking. 'Come on quicker, quicker, you swines.' Guns into our backs if we did not move quickly enough. On and on! It was snowing hard now. I had my arms locked into the arms of a Frenchman; he had been in my barrack at the Buna camp. (I have forgotten his name, but I think I owe my life to him, as you will see.)

I thought it looked funny somehow; like a lot of cattle or sheep we were being herded along. No one knew where we were going: all we knew was that we were fleeing from the Russians. The SS were fleeing too, but they could not go quicker than us; they had to guard us. On and on we went, throughout the night. Some of the men could not walk any more; they were slower and slower, and then they found themselves at the back of the queue of men, and then they separated off. Only to be shot by the watchful SS guards.

One man near me fell out to the side; I saw the SS guard take off his boots, so that he would freeze to death more quickly. Many went that way. Others I saw running away into the fields; then the SS guard would kneel on one knee, place his rifle to his shoulder and fire. Another one of us would not get home again.

My feet and legs were beginning to give out; I felt terrible. I told my French comrade and I slowed down considerably, but he started me up again. If I slowed down, he also slowed down because we had our arms locked together; he held onto me, dragging me along. Luckily I was the centre one of the five men; I tried again.

But in a little while I was going to give up; I could hardly lift up my legs, I tumbled over my feet; but the Frenchman held on to me. 'Come Leon,' he shouted, 'come on, comrade. We'll soon be there where we will have a rest. Come on now, Englishman.' And he dragged me along. My mind was still in good order. Whenever I saw the SS guards coming near me, I tried my best to make it seem all right, stepping on and on; then, as the guards fell behind doing a bit of checking up at the rear, I could feel my pains and aches, and started to slow down again.

One arm locked into my French comrade, one hand holding my piece of blanket and trying to keep up with the two men on my right. Feeling at a total loss, for I was on my way back to liberty, and now I felt like dropping and finishing this march.

Somehow I got fresh views and new strength; I pulled myself together and did well from then on.

It had stopped snowing, we had marched a huge distance, when we entered the little village of Nicolai. I remember seeing a little shop of Bata shoes and boot, and a church near by. The command was given: 'Halt!' At last we had stopped; it must have been midnight. I saw some of the men jump into dark doorways. Would they get away? We waited, it seemed about ten minutes, until the order was given to start marching again.

On and on; the snow-covered road; men falling out; men running away; men being shot; men being bullied, hurried along. Then we entered a brick factory along the road, and we were told to halt, and rest for a few hours. We climbed onto the wooden shelves; they were dusty, but we had a place to hang onto, and to get a little sleep. Drink? There wasn't any, there wasn't any food. Who cared? Just now I wasn't walking any more.

After a while we aroused each other, the order was given to get ready to march off again. The whole early morning, the whole day, marching, walking, on and on. Germans in little horse carts were rushing passed us, companies of marching SS men. They were running away from the enemy. We were feeling better for seeing this sight. Sometimes we slowed down, and then a farmer's wife would come to the door of her cottage, and some of us received some water. Until the SS guard came along to chase us away.

It was getting dark, and then I saw a road sign. It read 'Gleiwitz', a Polish town 90 kilometres from Cracow. We had marched a long, long way. Soon we neared the Gleiwitz concentration camp. We noticed that the camp was empty; it had been evacuated. Commands were given for us to get into the barracks and rest. Ah! here at last we could find some sleep, inside, out of the cold. But there were not enough barracks for the mass of men. It was a question of the strong being inside first. Many fights broke out and I walked out of a barrack, tried several others, but at every door there was a pushing and shouting and pleading. Somehow there was no room for all of us.

I walked around the barracks, and at last I placed myself on one of the steps of a building, tightened my blanket around me, and closed my eyes. I wanted to sleep. It was colder than before. I was losing bodily warmth, and, as I was dosing off, from somewhere a picture came into my mind: our men falling out of the marching column, and freezing to death. I realised I would freeze to death as had Max Stad at Birkenau. I would not wake up again if I stayed on the step outside in the icy wind. I picked myself up, and started to walk towards the barrack; my feet felt like cardboard; I could hardly move them. Somehow I got to the barracks, looked through a window, saw men lying in the bunks, around on the floor, piled on top of one another. I climbed through the window, let myself drop on to a heap of men. We were too tired to fight, and I managed to get a few hours' sleep.

The next morning the word went around that those men who could not walk would be allowed to stay behind. That was just right for me, no more marching, my feet were aching. And the Russians would soon be here, and I would be a free man again.

The men who could not walk had to present themselves at the barracks hospital for inspection. So I did; here I was face to face with Dr Silberman. He had seen me often at the hospital. He had told me then that I ought to try and understand that the men were like oranges and lemons; they were being pressed until nothing much was left over, and so it was dangerous to ever be in hospital. Now he told me that it would be dangerous to stay behind, for funny things would happen; he urged me to try to walk and not stay behind. I did not believe that the SS were going to shoot more of us, in the face of the Russians. They dare not kill us off, so I thought.

I was told to present myself to a barrack where the invalids were being held. Several hundred men were there already, and a few at a time were coming in. I was wandering around in the barrack among the men, ill-clad, hungry, poor in health.

I remember seeing a Dutchman: he was from Rotterdam, Mr Velleman, a pavement photographer, in his civilian life. But now he was standing there near a fireplace on which he had put a few pieces of bread to toast. His hand was bandaged and there was a bandage around his head. He seemed in good spirits. We talked while he was watching his bits of bread on the fire. I mentioned my suspicions about the SS killing off the men who could not walk; that they might not let us stay alive for the Russians to find us. I wandered off, and then I heard a tumult, and looked around. I saw my Dutch friend in a fight with others. I neared him, and asked what it was all about. He told me he had turned his head and in a second someone had stolen his toast from the fire.

While I was looking around the camp the day before, I had found a lovely silver spoon and a shaving brush, a razor, and a piece of shaving soap. The thought came to me that I could earn something to eat shaving the men in other camps on my way home. And the spoon would make a wonderful souvenir.

While I was walking about in the barrack a man jumped at me, and put his hands around my throat. He was shouting something I could not understand for he appeared to be of Greek nationality. I felt myself choking, and tried to get out of his closing hands and fingers. I thought I had had it when somehow some men separated us, and talked to the attacker. The man had thought I had pinched his piece of margarine; and I was thinking he had spotted my silver spoon, and was going to take it from me.

After a few hours a window of the barrack was opened, and an SS officer put his head through. He shouted out for us to be quiet and listen. He ordered out of the barrack 'all non-Jewish men of German nationality'. Some went out. Then he ordered out all non-Jewish Frenchmen; they went out, followed by other non-Jewish men. Only the Jews were left inside. I quickly spoke up to him, calling out: 'I am an English Jew.' He looked at me and shouted that I must have done something wrong, for I should not have been here; and with that he closed the window, and that was that.

There we were, hundreds of Jewish invalids of all nationalities. What was going to happen to us? I reasoned it out and concluded that I ought to try to get out of the cage. The SS had something bad in mind for us. I got outside the barrack, only to be confronted by the gun of the SS guard. He pointed it at me and I hopped inside again. I tried the other side of the barrack; out I went but another guard was standing near the barbed wire.

I could see hundreds of men on the other side of the wire and I called out to some of the men I used to work with. But nobody seemed to want to listen to me, or cared. Then I saw Carl, one of the foremen I used to shave in the barrack. He was always kind to me, he had a good nature. In my desperation I shouted out his name a few times: at last he saw me and came near to the wire. What was I doing inside there? I answered it was a mistake and that I wanted to get out.

To the SS guards Carl said: 'This man is a good labourer, he need not be in there.' The SS answered: 'Oh, what, the man cannot walk!' I shouted: 'Yes! I can walk, see here.' With all my might I jumped up and down a few times, and walked a little. The SS officer unlocked the gate, and I rushed out. I was ready to take up the next challenge, march or no march. I must get away towards home.

Then I stood face to face with an old friend of mine, who also came from Rotterdam. He was David Fierlier, a ginger-haired fellow. We were both so surprised we could not say much. I greeted him. He greeted me and asked me what I was doing there. I told him I had just got out of the death cage and, in turn, he told me that he was getting ready to march off with his group of men. We made a promise to see each other when we got back to Rotterdam. I never did see David again, nor photographer Velleman. They must have perished on the last lap home.

Rumours went that a rolling stock of trains would come into the Gleiwitz camp, and take all of us further away. I did not mind that, so long as it was further towards home. There must have been about 3,000–4,000 of us. Waiting all day long on the platform of the Gleiwitz station; SS guards watching us; all waiting for orders. Rations were handed out to each man; the usual piece of bread and the slice of sausage. But we saw the SS men receive a bigger ration of bread, and a large piece of sausage. It meant we were in for a long journey.

There we stood: the thousands of us, sick, tired, miserable, hungry, ill-clad, unhappy men. But hopeful, looking towards liberty. If we only knew where we were going! Patiently waiting, stamping our feet. It was cold; evening was nearing.

Then in the distance we saw a locomotive engine coming towards us, pulling about 30 railway trucks, mostly open coal trucks. It was getting darker; commands were given for everybody to get into the trucks. The guards shouted: 'Alles einstiegen, schnell!' The stronger men soon found their way onto the trucks, just like monkeys. But the weaker ones could not do this so easily. I was among these invalids: we were bullied and chased onto the trucks, and here and there a gun came down onto some of the men's backs.

At last the platform was empty. In my truck there were at least 140 men, all in a space only big enough to hold perhaps about 60. Still we had to make the best of it. A few of the strong men took it upon themselves to be our leaders. We tried various positions – standing, sitting, squatting – all seemed very unsatisfactory. Then we just let ourselves fall down on top of one another, three and four men high. This resulted in fighting, pushing, shouting going of for quite a while, while the train was travelling at a slow speed.

I did not fight: I could not do anything at all. I just sat in between two Dutchmen, both from Amsterdam, one of these men was my camp friend Barend Dinsdag. He was a nice chap, and often with me. Barend had known a way of exchanging my canteen cigarettes, which we could get once a month in the camp, for some bread: 20 poor-quality cigarettes for a half-loaf of bread, and he would bring me the food to share. Barend Dinsdag was only 5ft 2in tall, very optimistic indeed. He used to say often, over and over again, that the Boche would never kill him.

I was sitting all the time in one spot with knees up high. On my left was Barend Dinsdag, on my right the other tall Dutchman. I was feeling the cold, the hunger and the misery and pleased to be with a couple of friends so near by. The journey took five days, and during that time there was plenty of sorrow.

During the day we travelled very little, keeping away from the big towns, although sometimes we did pass under the bridge of a town. One early morning, the people on their way to work threw down into our trucks their packets of sandwiches, until they were shot at by the SS guards.

Every morning our dead comrades were taken down from the trucks, always four or five. They were the weak ones, who had suffocated or frozen to death. No food, no drink, all we had was a blanket tucked around us. Snow was falling most of the time. Life was unbearable. I developed a temperature; I was talking in my sleep. When awake I kept on repeating to my friend Barend that he must go to my parents' home in Rotterdam or get in touch with some of my family, and tell them that I had stuck it out and was alive on such and such a date, and that I did make a fight of it, but had to give up in the end. I felt so near to dying at times. Barend kept answering me: 'Yes, my friend, I will do so, I promise I will.'

We did not have any food or drink for three days. Then during the third evening we arrived at a station, and, as we halted, food was promised to us. Command was given that into each truck 25 loafs of bread would be thrown and the bread was to be shared, five men to a loaf. There they came into our truck, one after another. A terrible struggle took place; fighting broke out. I kept sitting where I was: I could not fight or struggle anymore, I did not care. If it was God's wish for me to perish here, all right I was accepting this. In any case, I would have lost my place, and then what would have happened? If I stayed where I was my friends could take up their positions again.

The strong got to the bread easily; the weak ones got very little; and the dying men needed none at all. Barend Dinsdag came away from the struggle with some large and small pieces of bread, the way it had been torn off from the loaves as the men fought for it. I got my piece of bread; it was sufficient for me.

Early the next morning, at about 2 o'clock, the train halted again; hot soup was promised to us. One bowl of soup to be shared by three men. Most of us had no bowl left because they had been used for other purposes in the truck, and then slung away. I did get up that time: hot soup is what I needed, something hot. I begged to one of the chaps to let me share in the hot soup; he did let me drink, it was very hot. I could not get it down me quickly enough. All this was taking place while standing in the trucks. Then the command was heard for the trucks to move off. I found my spot with my Dutch friends and on went the journey.

There was plenty of snow falling, and our blankets were covered. The men around me were using their spoons to get the snow off their blankets, and making a meal of it. I asked for a spoon full of snow. I was given none. I tried to get some off the blanket of a chap not far from me; he caught me and was going to hit me when my Dutch friend held him off.

Such beasts we were becoming, that for a bit of snow we would fight. In turn some of our men jumped from the truck whenever the train stood still in the fields, to fill up a metal container with snow from the ground, and so share it out among the other starving men. One day my turn came to climb down from the truck and fill the little metal containers with snow. I did not say no. I wanted to do my duty and cause no ill feeling.

I was busy with my spoon getting the lovely white snow into the container, not touching the yellow-coloured snow near the rails. I did not know what was going on around me. I had one thought in mind: fill this container up, and get back into the truck before an SS man catches you. All of a sudden I felt something hitting my back, the gun of an SS guard. He shouted at me: 'You dirty, swine. What are you doing there?' I turned and looked up at him, saying: 'We are hungry, give us something else to eat.'

He dragged me upright, and told me to help carry my comrades, pointing behind me. 'What comrades?' I thought. I looked around: there were other chaps carrying our dead comrades, who had died in the trucks. One long parade, their stiff dead bodies, blue, green, yellow and dirty black faces and hands. They did not hold out. They did not feel anything anymore!

I wanted to climb into the truck and partly succeeded, handing the nearly filled container to one of my comrades, and then I was pulled down by the SS officer. He had spotted me again and he forced me to get hold of the dead bodies and help to carry them to the last truck of the train. I did so; three or four men carrying one body. I did this journey a few times, but noticed the last truck was a large, covered one. I looked inside it, and saw many, many of our dead comrades, piled up across one another, just like loaves of bread.

I could not stand it any longer. My thoughts told me not to take part in this mass murder. I slipped around to the other side of the trucks. I saw no one on that side, and I made a run for it. As quickly as I could, I found my truck; I was helped inside and soon found my seat in between the two Dutchmen. I told them what I had seen, and then asked for my ration of hand-picked snow. There was none left, and I dared not go out and try again. Soon we moved off again.

One of the men – a Dutchman from Rotterdam, Jaap Theeboom – was going a bit haywire. I woke from one of my restless dreams and I found that he had one of my feet under his arm. I felt very uncomfortable like this, and I asked him to let go of my foot because my leg was going dead. He did not want to let go and he started to curse. I shouted at him. His son Joop pleaded with him and my Dutch friends told him to let go; finally he let go and I had my leg to myself again.

Then Jaap Theeboom made a nuisance of himself, and started to make trouble with others around him. He told us he was going to jump out of the truck and make a run for it. He'd be home sooner than the others, he shouted. I can still see him crawl over the men, heave himself up and disappear over the truck. I never saw him again. So near to freedom, but too late for him.

My feet were giving me a lot of concern; they ached too much now, and I took off my boots. The following morning I could not get them on again: my feet were twice as thick, ugly and swollen. And I was once again in a terrible condition. I knew it and my friends knew it too. Yet a little while longer, and I would have to say cheerio to this life.

10 Buchenwald

At last the train steamed to a halt. It was the fifth day and early in the evening, about 5 or 6 o'clock. We had stopped at the Buchenwald camp. The strong men jumped from the trucks onto the ground. The weak ones were helped down. The others just lay there and waited. I asked to be helped down; a prisoner of the Buchenwald camp obliged, he was dressed in a dark green coat. He was one of the camp police I was told later.

I called out for my friend Barend Dinsdag and in my fit of illness I asked him to try to carry me a little way. How foolish this request was. It was now every man for himself. But Barend did help me to stand up against the wall, where others were standing, and that was the last I saw of Barend Dinsdag. He did not get home.

I somehow made myself walk towards a door of the barrack building I was standing near: it was the bath house. I stood behind a mass of pushing and arguing men, who wanted to be let inside. Suddenly the door opened, and one of the camp police came rushing out swinging his baton. The mass of men moved back and I found myself on the ground being trodden upon. I shouted out: 'Help me, help me!' Then some hands picked me up and gestured to the door; I again walked up to it. The man behind the door saw me coming all by myself and he let me inside.

I was filthy from head to toe. I was told to take off my clothes which I gladly did. I had had enough. I did not care anymore for the silver spoon I had found at Gleiwitz. I did not care for the shaving brush or razor; nothing mattered now. I was inside out of the cold. I let my clothes fall to the ground. I was naked. I could hardly walk; never mind, I was inside, part of the nightmare was over.

I looked around me. The picture before my eyes made me think of an eel shop, and a container in which the eels crawl slowly around. Human bodies – men, skin and bones – were crawling around in all directions over the floor, trying to reach a water tap, which was dripping of the wonderful fluid. Some could make the journey to this sink, heave themselves up, let the drops of water get into their partly open mouths. Then they let themselves drop again to the floor, where they were helped further away to a suitable place. I wondered if this was going to do them any good, water to a body in this condition would kill. I asked the barber, who was cutting the hair of some of these men, if it wasn't dangerous for them to drink the water. He answered: 'No, they are as good as gone, so let them have their way.'

The barber was a Dutchman from Maassluis; he told me he had a hair salon there. I asked him what was going to happen to us all here, and if the weak ones would now be gassed as they were in the other camps. There were plenty of weak men from our train load. He looked at me and said: 'No, there is no gas chamber here. If the men are going to be killed off, why clean them up?' I was partly put at ease. The attendant was getting the baths ready. I shared a Lysol bath with several other men. Then we were laid down naked to dry. We were then led into another part of the barrack. The ones that could not walk were carried and placed on the floor. I noticed there were men lying down ready to leave this world. They were too weak to even move, but they were still breathing.

We were brought here to be registered: another number given to our names. It was a slow process because as some of the comrades could hardly say their names. While I was partly sitting, partly lying, I saw another queue of comrades passing us going into the bath house. They all looked dirty, tired and suffering. I noticed my friend Jacques de Wolf: I shouted out his name; he looked around and saw me, and called out my name: 'Ha! Leon!'

The registering of names and numbers had come as far as the men in front of me; I was told my number, 120 930; but no, no, not yet – the prisoner inspecting us saw the man in front of me move slightly. He was not yet dead, so he became 120 930. I became Buchenwald 120 931. After spending a few more hours at the registration, we were taken outside, and, because I could hardly walk, I was loaded with some others into a barrow and taken to another barrack.

These were large barracks, with bunks from top to bottom; each bunk had six or more spaces, each space about two foot high.

You could not sit up straight in these spaces, but had to lie down, or lean on one elbow to raise the body a little. One head was placed so that it faced the inside of the barrack, the next man had his feet facing the same way, the next man again his head outside; it looked like a bakery shop, loaves of bread having just left the oven.

It must have been about 9 o'clock in the evening. How mad it seemed to be lying down in a space not high enough to sit upright. I was glad to be inside. But I had not had anything to eat for the last few days; the hungry feeling came to me in all its eagerness, just as before, the body being safe for the present. My body now demanded food. And our prayers were heard. There before my eyes metal food containers were being brought in, and a ration of soup was given to each one of us. It was very hot and I could only sip it slowly. My comrade next to me had a shot wound in his cheek, and he could not feed himself properly. I saw his hopeless condition. He cried out softly, every time he took some liquid into his mouth. It ran outwards through the little puncture in his cheek. I suggested he turn over to the other side, and I poured some food into his mouth; it stayed inside, and he swallowed, and he was pleased. But he was too sick to finish his ration and told me to finish it for him.

From my bunk I had an interesting view. As I lay down and stared across to the opposite side of the barrack, I saw the bunk lowest to the ground was filled with the men almost dead, and very weak ones. The second tier was filled with the men that could only just climb into them; I was one of these. Then the third and fourth tiers were full of the more physically fit men, and they were pushed and squeezed very close together, on their sides.

At last sleep overtook us, and for the next few hours we did not know of our misery. The following morning about a dozen doctors came along to inspect us, and soon I saw many dead comrades being taken away, and the various wounded men sent to different parts of the camp hospital. I knew I was in an unfit state; my feet were bad; I had a wound to one of my hands. I thought I might be overlooked, so I made myself heard. One of the doctors took a look at my feet and hand, and, after treating my hand, he gave instructions for me to be taken away elsewhere.

I woke up, nature was calling on me. I slowly let myself slide from my wooden bed and my aching feet touched the muddy ground. I walked as best as I could, pushing the groups of men standing in my way, so that I had a clear space to walk; I was careful that no one should tread on my feet. It was a long walk before I reached the other end of the barrack. I had to get outside. I opened the door and found what I was looking for. The ground was covered in snow and mud. I had to walk in it and I hoped it would not harm my feet. They looked ugly, swollen and dis-coloured. I was well aware that I was in for trouble, but I was also on the way home.

I got back to my wooden boards and, listening to the sound of the many voices of the men talking, I soon fell asleep. I was taken to a department in the camp hospital where I was given another bath and then put into a bed.

The following morning, my feet were inspected by someone who I suppose was a medical man. I was told my feet had to come off. The doctors would operate on them when it was my turn. I told the male nurse who was also the head of the ward that I was a British national, that my problem was only chilblains, from which I suffered every winter. I did not want to have my feet cut off; they would heal as before. And the Americans would soon be here and I would be sent to England and be treated for this complaint.

Somehow, it seemed to make an impression on the man and he started to treat my feet with Vaseline; luck was with me once again. Every other morning my feet were treated in the same way, and somehow they healed nicely, except the big toe of my left foot: it was twice the size, and continued giving out dirty matter.

There were several men with the same complaint: bad feet because of the death march. Some had one or both feet amputated. The smell of those bad feet, which were only rotting away, was unbearable. There was a young Dutchman – his name was Appy Perils – who was not much older than 18. I remember him well: at Monowitz, he used to give boxing displays. The ginger-haired boy was now crying out from the pain of his feet, and I called out to him and started a conversation. He asked me to make his bed for him, when they took him away to amputate his feet. I did this, and, when he got back from his ordeal, he was unconscious. The following day he cried out, as he woke up to realise what had been done to him. He was to be a cripple for life. As the days

117

went by, we talked continually about the various things we would do when we got home again.

He mentioned he would never see his parents or sister again: they had been gassed at Birkenau. I suggested that he could not be sure of this. Anyhow, I still hoped to find my wife. He asked me where I had seen my wife and child for the last time. I related to him our arrival at Birkenau, the separation and then afterwards seeing her with the baby in her arms on a lorry with women. Appy stopped me then. The lorry loads of women and children, too sick to walk, were driven to the gas chambers. He said he saw masses of people go in but not one come out. He knew, he assured me, because he had worked not far from the gas chambers, and had seen it over and over again. My hope was dwindling, like snow in the sun, but I held onto the possibility of the unexpected.

I spent about a month in this hospital at Buchenwald. My feet were getting better. I was pleased I still had them, yet perhaps I was glad that my big toe was not responding to treatment like the rest. It meant I would have to remain in hospital. I was not going out into the open, out into the snow, cold and winds. I often thought about the possibility of further marches. I would not be able to march now, and then what would happen to me? I must try to remain well and alive, until liberation.

Every week half-a-dozen eggs were dealt out to some of the men in my ward. There were about 26 men in bed, also some Danish prisoners who were in poor health. They sometimes received Red Cross parcels, and then they sometimes gave me their midday soups. I watched them unpack their food parcels, what a wonderful sight. I never got an egg in the ward, perhaps I wasn't sick enough. But hunger was playing me up again and, after watching the Danish prisoners eat their home-made sausages and bread, I used to turn away, hide my face in the pillow and try to sleep.

I realised I was now on German soil, and thought perhaps my political status could be to my advantage. Thinking I might be removed to a better camp, being a British subject, I made up my mind to write down my history and have it brought to the attention of the German authorities.

A comrade in bed next to me was a Czech, but he could speak English and German. I asked him to translate into German what I was writing in English. I gave him my name, nationality, and my complaint of having been brought into the concentration camps by mistake; that I would like to be interned under the Red Cross.

After my friend had translated it all into German, I took care of the letter until the evening, when I noticed the male nurse taking up duty for the night. I knew he would come around from bed to bed, taking our temperatures, and so, when he came to me, I handed him my letter and asked him to hand it into the Political Department of Buchenwald camp.

He seemed surprised; he read the letter and looked at me with an insolent face. He made a gesture with the hands as if a noose was around the neck, and mine too; he tore up the letter and gave me one more look, as if to say I had better behave myself. I gathered that, if he had given the letter to the SS department we would both have been strung up.

I passed the time away, sleeping, talking, sleeping, hoping, trusting; and all the time I was hungry. I listened to the nightly air raids by the RAF or Americans, bombing the nearby towns.

At last I was told that I was to leave the hospital the following day. My feet seemed all right, I could walk again. I was in no happy state of mind. Being out in the cold again, a new camp, new conditions; and who knows what else? I did not like what was in store.

As the evening arrived I felt I had a temperature, but did not understand why. When the nurse came around he too was surprised. He asked me where I had a pain, if any? I answered that my ear felt a bit funny. He looked and said: 'You have erysipelas, a contagious disease.' I had to leave the hospital for another, directly the next morning.

I was placed in a wheelbarrow, and brought to another hospital. As I sat there waiting for a doctor to attend to me, I thought myself lucky to soon be in a warm bed again. I was far from well enough to work. I would not last long, and then, who knows what would happen to me?

A Russian doctor came to me, looked at my ear. I told him that I was an Englishman, from London. He took me for a Tommy, and called out to another doctor, telling him I was a Tommy. This doctor – Dr Albert Kongs from Luxemburg – spoke English to me. He asked who I was and why I was here, and so on.

He had been caught by the Germans while doing some resistance work for the Allies. He promised me that I would be with him in the hospital until liberation, as soon as the Americans arrived. It would be about three weeks, and then the Americans would have liberated the camp. I was pleased to have found a new friend; I was going to be looked after.

I was given a bed. I noticed the sheet was none too clean, and I dared to asked for a clean one: I was told that the clean washing had not yet come in, and so I was stuck with it a little longer. My toe received fresh bandages; my ear was painful, and I had to take tablets, and hope for the best. My hope and courage were growing again: soon this war was going to be over, and I'd be a free man.

Many men were suffering with the same illness as me. I remember a Belgium subject, a man from Ostende, his eyes were closing, and he thought he was going to stay blind forever. He wanted to die: he stopped eating, but I helped to feed him, and soon he was getting well again. He was quite a nice chap, about 40 years old. We became friends. I promised I would come and see him in Belgium, after liberation. He presented me with a pair of blue leather gloves: a wonderful present and souvenir, but someone stole them from me.

Many of the chaps died; dysentry was one of the many causes. I saw them struggle for air, and then slowly die. I use to say goodnight sometimes and the next morning they were dead; stiff, perhaps heart failure.

One day a slim Italian – Louigi Levi – came onto the ward. He was suffering with his stomach. His bunk was opposite mine. I saw him grow weaker and thinner, day after day. His food would not pass; I helped him by feeding spoonfuls of soup into his mouth. But soon it came back, and his situation was helpless. I was ordered by the *Kapo* to take him to the lavatories. Later on it wasn't necessary because no food went into his stomach. The remains of his soup went to me: I was entitled to this. There were no medicines, and nothing much could be done for the sick.

And I watched Levi fade away, like a dying candle; looking straight into his eyes, they were far away. Then Levi raised his arms and I watched his hands trying to fight off death itself. A very faint smile around his mouth; then his arms dropped. He lay still, very slowly his eyes lost their shine, and then he was gone from us. He had peace. Levi, Levi of Firenze.

I called the doctor, who had asked me to call him when it was over. Some of the chaps took away his body in a sheet. The *Kapo* came along and told me I could have Levi's ration of soup. I asked whether I could have his leather strap as a souvenir: I could and I still have it.

My friend Oscar Rotschield had the bunk next to me. He was a young German Jew, who with his family had left Germany and settled in Greningen, Holland. He had escaped the Nazis in Germany, but was caught again in Holland. Oscar was suffering from dysentry; he was as thin as a skeleton, just bones covered by skin. I helped him as much as I could: making up his bunk, taking him to the lavatories. Later on he could not even walk any more.

He made me take his ration of bread to a Frenchman, a non-Jew, who had received a Red Cross parcel, and I had to exchange Oscar's bread for a piece of gingerbread. Of course, I argued with Oscar that the gingerbread would only make him worse, but I did it for his sake. He was a very sick boy, but full of hope to get back to Holland. He gave me a letter when I left Buchenwald; it said that he would always be my friend, because of what I had done for him. I have this letter, and it makes me sad to think of the bad times poor Oscar and the other men went through.

Every other morning the chief surgeon came along the bunks, looking into the faces of the suffering sick. I usually pulled the blanket over my head, hoping he would not call me out of the bed, making him think that here was another body wasting away.

Orders were given by the SS commander, that all Jews had to assemble outside on the square. (Every barracks had a loud-speaker connected to the commander's headquarters, and so every *Kapo* heard the various commands and instructions which had to be carried out.)

From my bed I could see through the window into the barracks opposite. SS officers were shouting out: 'All Jews should present themselves.' But no one was seen or heard. The Jews knew the war was nearly over, and they did not want to be shot now. Mass killing was still taking place every day. The SS guards had their way of dealing with the situation. I saw them using their guns, shooting into the barracks several times. Then the doors of the barracks opened, some men rushed out down the stairs. A few of them fell, and the others came rushing down trampling on those who had fallen. About a dozen or so dead were lying there. They had been stamped upon.

Also in the various hospitals a check-up was made to find all fit Jews: they had to leave, and probably even the sick ones who could walk. Rumours had it that these unhappy ones were marched outside the camp and shot.

A young man went around from bed to bed in my ward asking the patients. 'Are you a Jew?' Then he would mark the paper in his hands. He reached my bunk; I had already thought what to say. I answered him: 'I am a half Jew, and that was marked down on his sheet. I hope God has forgiven me for using this plan to save my life: half Jews had a kind of privilege.

It was now well into April: all fit and able men were taken away and finished off. I asked the doctor whether I could change places with my Italian friend who had died that day, suggesting that my number and name would go to the dead man, and I could take his number and name.

But the doctor thought it not such a good idea, he told me that everybody had to leave the camp. All those who could walk, even himself, were expected to leave soon, if the liberators did not come. The SS commander had promised to hand over the Buchenwald camp with all its inmates to the Americans when they arrived, but he did not keep his promise. Men were being killed off, right to the very end.

But the liberators did come, only just in time to save the rest of us.

11 Liberation

It was 11 April 1945, everything seemed so quite inside and out-side the barracks. I stood in front of the window and looked out-side. There wasn't a soul to be seen. Even the SS watchtowers were empty. The guards were not there; the SS was escaping.

A small aeroplane was circling over Buchenwald camp; it was about 4 o'clock in the afternoon. Next to the window, but too far for him to see out, was the bunk of my friend Oscar Rotschield; he was too weak to walk or even stir himself. There before my very eyes was the most exciting picture I had seen for a long time. A picture I will never forget.

Groups of our own comrades were appearing from the dis-tance and marching between the barracks. Some were carrying guns on their shoulders, others had large white sheets, and were placing these on the roof tops. Within minutes there was an excit-ing shouting and orders were heard. This was the moment all of us had waited for, for such a long, long time.

I was free. We were free! I gave Rotschield a running com-mentary on the events. 'We are free, boy. Free!' He joined in with me as well as he could. He was beginning to see his wishes come true, but alas only partly. Oscar Rotschield did get back to Holland, but only as far as Eindhoven, where he died. This sad news reached me when my letter to him was returned. I seem to have lost many interesting comrades at the very last; either through sickness or at the hands of the SS.

General Patton's 3rd Army liberated Buchenwald on 11 April at approximately 4 o'clock in the afternoon, only just in time. The army saved 21,000 men from being killed. Berlin had given instructions for every barracks to be blown up: to destroy Buchenwald with the inmates.

I was free, but did not leave my place at the hospital barrack for the next two days. I had to see to my clients: the doctor, the

Kapo, they needed a shave. Perhaps I did not yet understand that I could go out and come in as I wished.

But I did make the effort: some clothing was given to me and out I went in search of the Americans. I shook hands with the first GI standing near his jeep. I spoke to him, told him who I was; he was surprised to hear his own language, for most of the prisoners around him were Poles, Russians, Dutch and so on. The soldier asked me if I would like some biscuits. I answered: 'Yes, please.' And, as he made a move and got the packets of biscuits out of the back of his jeep, like mad men, everybody rushed forward and in no time the biscuits were gone.

I presented myself to the American commander of the camp, and told him who I was and that I wanted to go home. He assured me that there was no hurry, and that I was now in good hands, and I should call back in the morning.

I wandered about from one place to another; visiting the ovens where the bodies of our fellow inmates had been cremated; inspecting the various articles connected with the punishments dealt out to the prisoners. I saw the heaps of dead bodies, the heaps of bones, ashes. (I even took some of the bones as tokens of remembrance.)

The following morning I left my barracks again, and happened to run into my friend Jacques de Wolf. I was very pleased to see him. I had one cigarette on me, which I had received from an American soldier. I had intended to give it to my friend the doctor, but I handed it to de Wolf.

Wandering about I met a GI in one of the SS barrack. I was looking for some food, and he was trying to find a spot to throw his bit of steak. I forgot my pride and asked him: 'You are going to throw this away, are you?' 'Yes,' he answered, 'it's as tough as the soles of my boots.' I asked him if he minded if I ate the steak, since I had not seen or ate a steak for about three years.

'Sure,' he said. 'Here you are, sit down and have it. I want to see you eat it.' He watched me all the time, and when I had finished the steak and fried potatoes, he asked me if I wanted any more. 'Yes,' I said, thinking he was making a joke; but he told me to come along to the kitchen part of the barrack. Soon I was sitting down eating yet more food.

The word went around that I could sing: I had told some of the soldiers about my life in the camps and that I used to sing for some extra food. I was asked by Captain Jacobs whether I could get up a kind of a concert for the boys that evening! This I promised, and off I went to find some other chaps to join in with me. I found a violinist, and another could play the saxophone; these instruments were found somewhere in the camp, but I could not find a piano. The concert was a success. There must have been about six or seven of our fellows giving their best, and the rations of food given to us by the Americans were appreciated. I had about a dozen different kinds of food.

The tin rations of the American soldiers seemed to be quite heavy. I was pleased when I reached my barrack. It was about 10 o'clock; everything was dark, and I sensed the new feeling of freedom; no one to jump on me, or to tell me off. But I did not want to take liberties by coming in late, and disturbing some of the comrades.

I got as far as my bunk, when a voice of one of the inmates whispered loudly: 'Englander! Leon what are you doing there, coming in so late?' It was the young tailor from the bunk opposite me. I went over to him and told him where I had been, and what I had been doing. He asked me for something to eat. Handing him a tin of rations, I promised him more tomorrow.

The following morning I was out and about early, wandering around the camp. I spoke to various GIs, and one in particular; he was on guard near a heap of black leather jackets, leather belts and heaps of guns, and so on – all SS property.

I told him that the Boche had taken away everything from me and that I would not mind having one of the leather jackets. He agreed with me, told me to go ahead and fetch myself one, and to bring one for him. I looked at him and asked if he was going to shoot me if I did take a jacket. He looked at me and assured me that he was not there to shoot any of us, and urged me to go and pick out two of the jackets and belts.

So I did. The jackets were new. I tried several for size, and, having made my choice, I picked out one for my soldier friend. Then I moved to the heap of SS leather straps and belts, and I took one of them. It would serve me as a symbol of remembrance. I took the second jacket to the American guard, thanked him, and went on my way.

In the evening I entered by barrack, took the leather jacket to the young tailor, and asked him whether he could sew on some other buttons because I did not want to wear the SS swastika buttons which were there. My comrade told me to get some other buttons; he had none; and his fee would be 3 litres of soup. I promised him 2 litres and he agreed.

Off I went in search of the clothing barracks or warehouse. I found the place, got inside through the window, and looked around. There were a lot of clothes, all kinds: they had belonged to others who were no more. I went through the garments to find my buttons; at last I found some and took them to my comrade the tailor. He told me my jacket would be ready the next day. I still have it; also a packet of Phillip Morris cigarettes, given to me at Buchenwald by the Americans. I have a little earth from the Buchenwald concentration camp; the spoon I used to eat with, and more.

The day arrived when I had permission to leave Buchenwald concentration camp, having received an identity card. I was told I could fly to England or France, just as I wished. I could not yet go to Holland because the fight was still on. I was given a paper, upon which was typed an order for me to be taken out of Germany by air.

There were several air fields around the camp, among them Erfurt aerodrome, but how could I get there? It was quite a long way to walk, and so I started looking around for someone to drive me there. I spoke to an American soldier as he was sitting in his jeep about the possibility of him taking me to an aerodrome. He was sorry that he wasn't going to any airfield; I had to try my luck elsewhere. I wandered off, and then a jeep pulled up almost next to me and its driver called out: 'Hey there, are you the fellow that wants to go to an aerodrome?'

'Yes, that's me,' and I noticed a lady in the jeep, next to the soldier. She made herself known as a journalist on one of the London papers. It was Miss Anne Matheson, from the *Evening Standard*. She wanted to know about what had happened to me, the camp, and so on. I told her I'd tell her some things, if she would put my name and London address in the article, so that my family in England would know that I was still alive and on my way home. She agreed and that must have been the first that my family heard about me for a long time.

It took another few days before I found myself driven to an aerodrome, I wandered about the field, spoke to various American soldiers, and then presented myself to the commanding officer. He inspected my papers, and I was allowed to wait until a plane could take me to France. I wanted to get to Holland, before England, because I needed to find out about my parents and others. Most of the flights were going to England, and I spent the night at the aerodrome.

It was evening, I was going from barrack to barrack on this airfield. At one of them I found myself with some American soldiers; they were just about to open a bottle of wine and I had to join in just to forget my troubles. I thought I could stay with them; I had not yet found a place to sleep; but no one offered help and so I partly staggered outside, after saying good night.

It was very dark. I started to walk slowly and I found myself swaying slightly … I never could stand drink, and I was drunk. As I walked on and on, I suddenly saw the shadow of a soldier coming towards me; he had his gun pointing at me and demanded to know what I was doing out here. I tried to tell him who I was, and so on.

He took me to his commanding officer who was fast alseep in bed. I was told to sit down and wait. He turned out to be the same officer who had seen me during the afternoon, and he was surprised that I was still here. He did not sound very friendly, I had been the cause of him losing his sleep.

After a while the door opened and in came about four or five British prisoners of war. They had been called for, and told to find out who I really was. I was interrogated by one of them, and I had to answer questions about London etc. I felt insulted, because they did not think all was right with me; perhaps I was a spy, an ex-Nazi or whatever. I seemed to have satisfied the men; the American commander told the British that they were responsible for me, and I had to share a place in their barracks.

I felt mighty proud to be lying there among my own people. How often had I thought of this, when I was still a prisoner of the Nazis. To crown it all I started to speak aloud, and some of the others told me to shut up, because they wanted to get to sleep. At last I also fell asleep.

The following morning, everybody was up and about, for the men would be taken to England by plane. I could come along if

I wished, but I told them I wanted to go to Holland, and for that I had to go to France first. Rations were shared, and I stood in a corner because I had no right to their rations. But they insisted that I got something. As I saw the men enter the plane and take off for England, I once again found myself alone.

I turned around to wander about, and I was face-to-face with an American guard. He asked me: 'Are you the one I took to the CO last night?' I answered: 'Yes.' He told me then that if I had not stopped and turned to him last night, he would have shot me, because he had already called out to me twice before, but I had not taken any notice, and had kept on walking. His orders were to stop anybody moving about on the airfield after 10 o'clock at night. I had escaped once again, my guardian angel was still with me.

During that afternoon, I was lucky to get a plane to Paris. It was an interesting trip. My first flight and the GIs and officers using the same plane were very friendly; asking me all about life in the concentration camps.

Arriving at the canteen of the aerodrome, I sat at the same table as the officers and men. They gave me coffee, and there was a big tray of doughnuts. I was told to eat as many as I liked, and I did, having only had a very small breakfast that morning. I put some into my pockets; I never knew when I would eat again.

After a while I was driven into Paris, and delivered to the British embassy. It was about 6.30 in the evening. A few questions were asked; and then nothing more, silence. It was near midnight when the busy gentleman in the room, asked me if I was hungry? About half an hour later I heard his phone conversation; I was being taken to a house in Paris for British subjects on their way to England.

I found myself at about 1.30 in the early morning, eating fried potatoes and greens, and drinking tea while talking to the owner of the house. I was given a room, a clean bed; I was becoming more and more human again.

The next morning I was up, and downstairs for breakfast. The room was filled with about a dozen people, seated at tables. I looked around and noticed an empty table in the far corner. I felt a stranger, and so I seated myself at this table. Then it happened.

A lady was coming over to my table; she asked me if I needed any help, and if she could pour out my tea. 'Yes,' I answered, and told her that she was the first woman to do so for me. She had noticed my short hair, and gathered where I had been. Yes, Louise Wyeth was a kind lady to me; she was on her way to England; she had been a nurse in France during the war.

I made my way on foot to the British consul; I needed a valid passport to travel to Holland. After the usual questions and answers, I was told that I had to wait to go to Holland; the war in Holland wasn't over yet.

I walked back to the British home and told my new-found nurse, Louise that my foot was hurting me in no little way. She had a look at it and told me to promise her that I would go to the British hospital, not far from the home. She was getting ready to leave for London. I asked her to visit my family, and give them first-hand information about me. We both kept our promises.

I visited the British Hertford Hospital in Paris and, after an interview with the medical officer in charge, Dr Swartz, I was persuaded to go into the hospital for a check-up, which ended with the amputation of the big toe on my left foot. Hitler did get a little piece of me after all.

I was very kindly treated by the nursing staff and began to regain my health. A French family came to visit the British patients regularly, and I found really good friends in Monsieur and Madame Gaston Pron with whom I stayed for several months. Their kindness and good cooking almost got me back to normal health. The many friends I found in Paris; the kind things they did for me, I shall never forget.

Then, at last, I was given permission to travel to Holland, where the misery had started. I was among many men and women who had been in the camps of the Nazis arriving at Eindhoven, and then the last bit of the journey to Rotterdam.

I was alone, no wife, no son, little else and robbed of most things. It was 10 October 1945, in the evening. I had been away three years and two days. I found my father and step-mother at the old address. My father knew I was on my way to him because I had corresponded with him from Paris. He was the first of the family that I held in my arms, after all this time.

My father had been in Westerbork, but was sent home after some 12 months because he was married for the second time to a non-Jewess American national. He was very frail, the Nazis had killed lots of Dutch people with hunger. In my search for my family I found that most of the Dutch side did not survive: more than 60 had gone away, only four are alive, one nephew and three cousins.

I had asked for milk from the Red Cross. It was advertised in the papers: people coming back from the camps could get extra milk. I wanted to give it to my father. The Red Cross sent me a letter saying I was refused milk because I was not a Dutch national, I was British. In 1942 we were not accepted as British but as Dutch Jews. In 1945 we were British and so did not qualify for free milk. What a miscarriage of justice, and one in which my wife and beautiful baby son were the victims.

From information received from the Red Cross it appears that of the transport of 700 people that left Holland for Auschwitz that day, only two men got back, after nearly three years. They were Leon Borstrock and myself.

It is difficult for me to know who exactly is to blame for the death of my wife and child and for my suffering. There were so many men involved that I can never hope to bring to justice the men I hold directly responsible: Else, Barney and I, as British subjects, should have been interned, under Red Cross protection. But we were not and I hold the following men responsible for what happened to me, and, foremost, for the loss of my wife, child and sister.

I accuse:

Mr Prodillier, the Swiss consul
Delayed the time of forwarding my completed forms with photographs to the British embassy in Bern. If he had acted responsibly for British interests, valid papers for internment of my wife, child and myself would have been received earlier, and in time.

Mr Roos, inspector of the alien police department, Rotterdam
Did not wish to help me in any way with the establishment of British nationality, and our rights to be interned as British subjects although he told me personally in the corridor at his station that

he knew I was British, but he wasn't going up against the wall for my sake.

Mr de Groot, of Rotterdam town hall
Did not take much notice of the notes and quotations on the card indexed under our name in his department.

Kurt Schlesinger, chief of Westerbork camp
Threatened to send me to Auschwitz on one occasion; refused to review our case for British nationality, and told SS commander Gemmeke that our case had been refused at The Hague. Told us we must go with the transport, but as he got back to his office, after the train had left the camp, he opened the morning mail and found a letter telling him of our nationality, and that we should be interned. This man should have opened his mail before the transport left. Had he done so, my wife and child and I would have been interned, and, under normal circumstances, my wife and child would have been with me now. Mr Schlesinger did hold back from a transport a Dutch subject and business associates; why could he not keep back British subjects?

I managed to make a new start in life after I returned to England on 22 November 1945. In the first few weeks, I was taken in by my brothers Morry and Charlie and their families. It was a shock to everybody in my family when Morry died on 7 December. I had been home just over two weeks. He left a wife and four children. As I was standing over the body of my brother, I promised I would try to help Dolly and the children. There wasn't much money between our families. The council gave me a weekly payment of 35 shillings which did not help very much.

I took the bull by the horns and continued where my brother left off. With my sister-in-law Dolly, I continued working the London markets such as Petticoat Lane where Morry had a trading licence for Sundays. We travelled the markets, sometimes working further away in the Midlands, Wales, the north – wherever I could get to earn a few bob. Travelling by train, or mostly by coach because it was cheaper, carrying two suitcases of goods such as ladies' hair curlers and wigs, I made money wherever I could; staying away from home months at a time, returning to London only when I had sold out, sharing the profits with Dolly.

Eventually Morry's two girls and two boys grew up and I moved into digs. My help wasn't needed any more because the boys were doing very well and the girls married and had families of their own. I worked the markets for over 40 years, never making a lot of money but earning a living all the same. I retired when I was 60, and now at 90 I still feel fit and healthy.

This book was a chance to tell my story and fulfil the promise I made to God all those years ago in the camps: if I survived, I would tell the world of the evil of the Nazis so no further generation could repeat the mistake. After lecturing in schools, colleges and universities for the last 50 years, warning of the evils of racism, telling people of my experiences, and now completing my story in this book, I feel I have fulfilled my promise.